AF544787

Leading Chaos

An Essential Guide To Conflict Management

Revised Edition

Alexandria A. Windcaller

zoomOpzoom Productions
P.O. Box 191
Wendell, MA USA 01379
www.zoomopzoom.com

Cover Design by Alexandria A. Windcaller and Michael Ruocco
Copyedited by Rosie Pearson
Printed by The Highland Press

International Standard Book Number (ISBN): 978-0-615-39507-4

Library of Congress Control Number: 2010935526

In Memory of My Maternal Grandparents

and

For all those in crisis who are unable to help themselves

CONFLICT/CRISIS MANAGEMENT GOALS		
Crisis *Prevention* Goal	⟶	Keep the Scene Safe
Crisis *Intervention* Goal	⟶	Make it (Myself and Scene) Safe
Crisis *Resolution* Goal	⟶	Confirm Scene Safety

Ten Tips for Re-directing Conflict

1. Say a Lot by Saying a Little
2. Silence
3. Acknowledge Emotions
4. Take One Step at a Time
5. Set the Pace
6. Be Mindful of Words that Incite
7. Actively Listen
8. Avoid Objectifying Yourself
9. Tell It Like It Is
10. Create Opportunities

The Response Crisis Intervention Model's
Goal-Oriented Intervention
is developed by
Alexandria A. Windcaller.

Response Training Programs
Website: www.responsetrainings.com
Email: info@responsetrainings.com

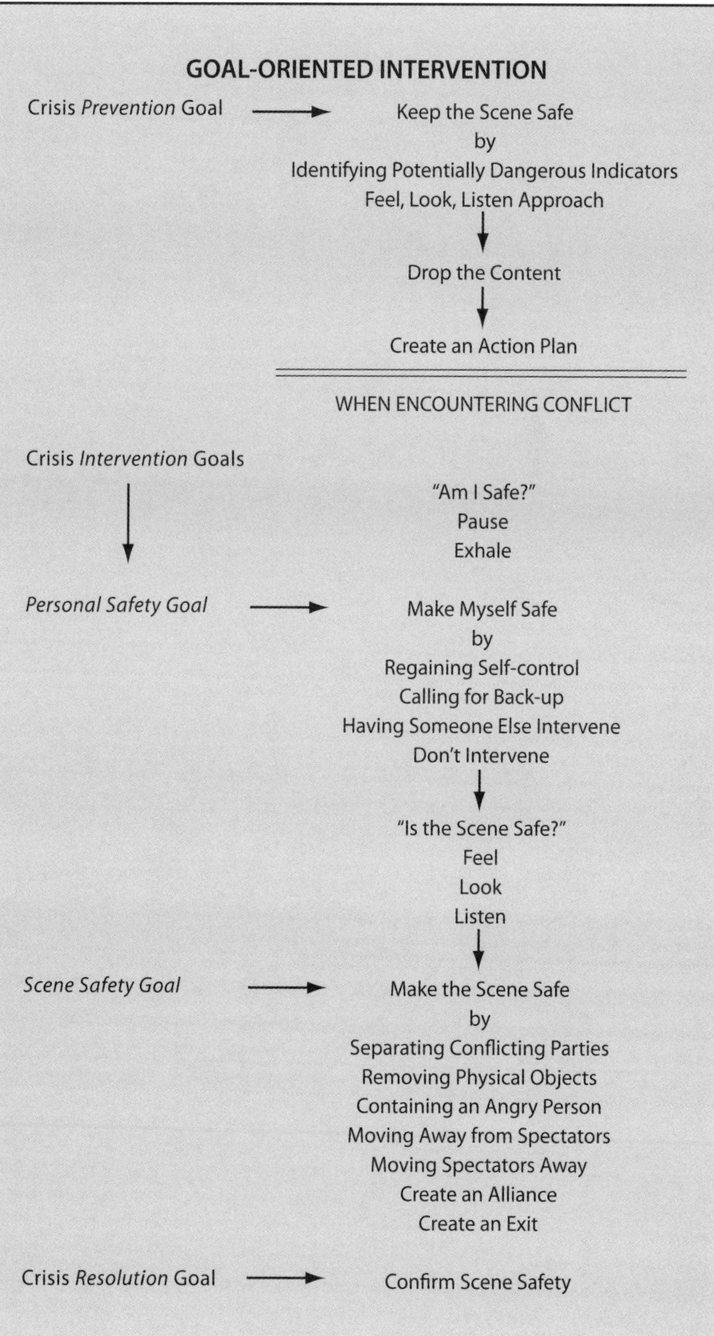
GOAL-ORIENTED INTERVENTION
Crisis *Prevention* Goal
Keep the Scene Safe
by
Identifying Potentially Dangerous Indicators
Feel, Look, Listen Approach
Drop the Content
Create an Action Plan
WHEN ENCOUNTERING CONFLICT
Crisis *Intervention* Goals
"Am I Safe?"
Pause
Exhale
Personal Safety Goal
Make Myself Safe
by
Regaining Self-control
Calling for Back-up
Having Someone Else Intervene
Don't Intervene
"Is the Scene Safe?"
Feel
Look
Listen
Scene Safety Goal
Make the Scene Safe
by
Separating Conflicting Parties
Removing Physical Objects
Containing an Angry Person
Moving Away from Spectators
Moving Spectators Away
Create an Alliance
Create an Exit
Crisis *Resolution* Goal
Confirm Scene Safety

Contents

Simplify Conflict....1
To Prevent....11
Am I Safe?....39
Is the Scene Safe?....53
Creating Order....79
Don't Forget to Breathe....110
Cause No Harm....132
The Model Relies on the Messenger....158
Acknowledgements....163
About the Author....164

Illustrations

Conflict Management Goals....i
Ten Tips for Re-directing Conflict....i
Goal-Oriented Interventions....ii

Goal-Oriented Intervention charts appear on Pages 11, 36, 44, 49, 53, 54, 63, and 90.

Simplify Conflict

You gain strength, courage, and confidence by every experience in which you really stop to look fear in the face. You must do the thing you think you cannot do.

— Eleanor Roosevelt

I am and will likely always be a reluctant authority in the field of conflict management. This line of work can mean a lot of different things depending upon whom you are speaking to. For myself, it means teaching what to do when faced with an emotionally charged and potentially violent incident. This wasn't a career that I was actively pursuing, at least not in the beginning. Fate has played an important role in my life.

The first conflict management program I took part in was at Long Lane School in Middletown, Connecticut, a minimum and maximum security facility for adolescents. "The Lane," which has since closed, was a treatment/correctional program for males and females between the ages of eleven and eighteen. All of the residents were sent there by the court system for crimes ranging from minor misdemeanors to murder. I was twenty-one years old, fresh out of college, with no background whatsoever in psychology, social work, or corrections. That didn't matter; my new position as an outdoor educator in the Youth Challenge program was a dream come true for me.

I was hired to manage an on-site ropes course and facilitate teambuilding programs for the residents. During the summer, I worked with a co-instructor, taking the teens on canoe trips down the Connecticut River and on overnight backpacking trips to the Appalachian Trail in northwest Connecticut. Working so closely with young criminals dictated the need to seriously hone my skills in conflict management.

A year after beginning this job, I was asked to participate in a new program being introduced at Long Lane called The Humane Process of Defense and Control. This was a crisis intervention program for staff members who managed potentially volatile people, and was based on a federal corrections model, that emphasized physical management of volatile behavior. My former supervisor was less than pleased when she found out that I had signed on while she was out on vacation. I was to become an instructor, and teaching crisis seminars was going to take a big chunk of my time away from my outdoor teachings. The administrators of our facility, however, were genuinely pleased to have a woman participating in the all-male instructor-training program. Having a woman as a lead instructor complemented Long Lane's unwritten policy that all staff, regardless of gender, could physically intervene and manage a crisis.

It quickly became apparent to me, however, that the program was one-sided and dangerous, with an emphasis only on physical intervention and barely a mention of verbal de-escalation. The physical techniques used pain compliance to coerce a person to submit. Without a more balanced approach toward conflict management that integrated verbal intervention and safe physical management techniques, the program was destined to fail. Besides, I really wasn't interested in a career in corrections. What I really wanted to do was scale tall mountains and spend my time in the outdoors—hiking, biking, and rock climbing. I quit my state job a couple of years after becoming certified to teach the Humane Defense course. I became self-employed and started designing outdoor gear under my own label. I looked forward to a life far away from locked doors and angry people. Fate, though, had other plans.

Within a year of pursuing my new enterprise, I was asked to work as a consultant to the state of Connecticut. The Department of Children and Families needed help integrating the Humane Defense program into five additional facilities. These sites included acute psychiatric hospitals and residential treatment centers. Even though I disagreed with the philosophy, I signed on to what I thought would only be a temporary position.

Meanwhile, I began researching alternative methods of conflict management and envisioned a program emphasizing verbal de-escalation skills. At the time, I lived ten miles from the Yale University Medical Library. I'd get a day pass and read through every abstract and book I could find on the topic of crisis intervention. There wasn't much written about verbal de-escalation back in the early eighties. Crisis intervention training was just starting to be recognized as a good idea for sites that served potentially volatile people. The Humane Defense program after all was considered a state of the art program at the time, even though it taught no verbal de-escalation.

The best part of becoming a Humane Defense Instructor for me was getting introduced to Aikido. Most of the physical management techniques in the program were derived in part from this Japanese martial art. I didn't know it at the time, but fate had just locked me into a very long study of a little know martial art that embraces joyfulness and kindness.

Aikido does not use strikes or kicks to subdue an attacker. Aikidoists learn to blend with an attack. For instance, instead of blocking a punch, which requires a great deal of physical strength, you allow the hit to go through. This means if you are on the receiving end of the punch, you have to learn how to step off to the side of the strike. The person delivering the punch will typically throw his full weight behind the hit, and thus fall slightly off balance if he doesn't make contact with your body. When a person is just off center, leaning too far forward after his punch, he can be easily moved without the need for brute force.

Verbal arguments are, metaphorically speaking, the same as physically blocking a punch. Loud and forceful arguments usually end with only one victor. Blocking another person, whether physically or verbally, sets up the same combative dynamic. Instead of blocking another person's viewpoint, you could figuratively step to the side of a disagreement, just as when stepping off the line of a strike in Aikido. Practicing a non-reactive approach toward conflict reduces your chances of becoming the target of another person's anger. Such a vantage point provides breathing room for both parties to seek nonviolent alternatives for working through a dispute.

In Aikido, the goal is to lead a dispute towards a safe conclusion and not to annihilate an attacker. I interpret the philosophy of this art as learning to see the higher self in even the angriest person. The higher self within the angry person can listen to reason, wants to be seen, not judged, and wants to feel safe. Speaking to an attacker's higher self creates an opportunity to avoid violence. It is a simple gesture, yet it is a novel technique. It takes people by surprise when you don't meet a violent interaction by becoming violent yourself.

Learning to fall safely into a roll is also a key component of this art. Over the course of an hour-long practice, you may roll forward or fall backward into a roll over a hundred times. Once you learn how to roll safely, being thrown across the room isn't a big deal anymore and is actually a lot of fun. That might not sound like your cup of tea, but haven't we all experienced a physical fall or emotional fall at least once in our lives? Aikido provides the opportunity to practice getting up from a fall with a smile on your face and a readiness to take on the next challenge.

Try as I may to describe Aikido, it still feels like I'm saying you can experience the Grand Canyon by standing at the rim and looking down. Rangers and seasoned hikers both know that the Grand Canyon needs to be hiked down along a trail to get a sense of the immensity of the canyon. Aikido is like the canyon. To fully appreciate what Aikido offers in the way of providing alternatives to meeting violence with greater violence, try some of the techniques mentioned in this book.

In 1983, I became a Humane Defense Instructor and expanded my studies into the art of Aikido. In 1990, my Aikido teacher or Sensei encouraged me to open a school, or dojo, near my home. Wendell Aikido is a traditional dojo that emphasizes ways in which to bring Aikido into our daily lives. Although the techniques presented in this book are not necessarily Aikido techniques, they are philosophically in sync with Aikido, The Way of Peace.

In 1986, I introduced the Response Crisis Intervention Model. This training model emphasizes verbal intervention as the primary conflict management tool. Though my research at the Yale library certainly informed me, I based the Response Model off of my experience in emergency medical assistance. Response, it should be noted, also teaches hands-on techniques derived from Aikido, but unlike Humane Defense, it does not use pain compliance.

The Response Crisis Intervention Model has been implemented in public schools, alternative correctional facilities, and human service agencies. Since 1986, I have worked with people and agencies in every walk of life from the United States Navy to local chambers of commerce. I also began writing articles for *Aikido Today Magazine* in 2000. My column, which ran for five years until ATM stopped its publication, was called "Off the Mat." It explored the use of Aikido-based principles in everyday situations and de-escalation techniques during conflicts.

I will always remain a bit conflicted about my role as one who teaches crisis intervention skills. Although I have accepted my role in this field of study, I truthfully wish that there were a decreasing need for this type of work instead of an increasing need to learn how to manage extremely volatile situations.

Many of the scenarios found in this book are based upon my own life experiences as an intervener. What I learned from those experiences is that the basic goals of conflict management are universal, regardless of the circumstances. It is my hope that you can use the skills detailed in this work to help keep yourself safe and help those who cannot help themselves.

About This Book

Choosing to seek nonviolent alternatives to managing conflict takes a lot of courage. It means accepting personal responsibility for your actions, not passing judgment onto others and controlling a "get even" inclination. The techniques described in this work run counter to the "might makes right" mode of conflict management so pervasive in our society today.

This book provides a systematic approach to safely manage conflicts whether you are a professional or nonprofessional crisis intervener. This approach is called the Goal-Oriented Intervention and it provides the baseline protocol for interveners utilizing the Response Crisis Intervention Model. Through a Goal-Oriented Intervention, you will learn to simplify the management of everyday quarrels and flash-point conflicts.

How to Read This Book

Antagonistic, disruptive, volatile, or threatening behaviors and quarrels between groups are examples of conduct that needs to be managed and redirected. Conflict management takes place daily in homes, offices, public schools, alternative schools, residential treatment centers, hospitals, and correctional facilities, as well as in other locales.

A societal tendency to compartmentalize work sites and workers promotes a segregated view of conflict management. Regardless of where you work or with whom, you can use techniques introduced in this work. Parental concerns are included.

For the most part, when I have used the word "client," it designates a person (not the intervener) involved in the conflict. If the scenario doesn't appear to coincide with your circumstance, however, you can change it to meet your own needs. For instance, if it says "The client was standing in the hall yelling" and you are not a clinical worker, put in your own designation: "The student," "my son," or "the agitated woman."

The term "intervener" is used throughout the book. By definition, this intervener is any person who chooses to manage a conflict. It does not necessarily imply that the person is working in a professional capacity. Some cases will be noted, however, with a reminder that a technique is meant especially for a professional intervener.

Over the past thirty years, the category of service that falls under the title crisis intervention has been ever-growing to include: disaster preparedness, suicide prevention, rape counseling, crisis hot lines, and fire safety, among many others. This book is about quarrels that can escalate into full-blown conflicts and are thus, from time to time, identified within this work as conflict-crisis.

The Burden of Conflict

What causes conflicts? Miscommunication, fatigue, and stress are everyday factors that can fan the flames of dispute. Every conflict scenario is unique due to the key characters involved and the ways they relate to core issues of their particular conflict. Individually, each of us can make a difference in how conflict will play itself out.

A conflict does not need to be complex itself in order to have a powerful impact on those involved. At minimum, a person may experience hurt feelings and an unwillingness to pursue resolution. Unfortunately, explosive behavior and physical violence have become increasingly commonplace.

When a conflict escalates to the point that confusion, lack of direction, or loss of self-control are experienced, there is chaos. The resulting crisis can have disastrous effects on all involved.

By and large, most people learn their approach to conflict early in life. Despite its predictability, people get overwhelmed and lose sight of why and how a conflict got started in the first place. Instead of moving through a dispute and seeking resolution, people in conflict tend to get stuck in a crisis mode.

Fight-or-Flight and the Unwarranted Power Granted to Conflict

A person may experience a desire either to join in and fight back verbally or physically or to seek to flee the scene. When one's rational self has been consumed by events at hand, emerging conflict takes on momentum with seemingly supernatural powers.

"I don't know what got into me."

"I just couldn't stop myself."

"Something inside of me snapped!"

"He went ballistic. I didn't recognize him!"

"Everybody joined in and started chanting 'Fight! Fight!'"

It is all too common for people to use conflict as an excuse for their failure to exercise self-control. Conflict is not an entity. If it were, managing its movement and impact would be easier. We could say to conflict, "Ah! There you are. I can see you. Get out of this house right now!"

Dismantling conflict's reign over people's actions begins with revealing the source of its power.

Conflict Makes People Feel Unsafe

To be safe means to be free from the threat of danger, harm, or loss. These three elements are at risk whenever you engage in a conflict.

A conflict that escalates into a physical confrontation, such as a fistfight, is undeniably dangerous. Physical harm is the extreme outcome of this type of conflict. You don't need to feel physically threatened to be in danger, however. Conflict can trigger an emotional response, thereby creating a state of vulnerability. Loss of emotional control and the unpredictability of conflict impact the degree to which people feel safe. Potential conflict is enough to make capable people avoid intercepting even small disputes.

Simplify Conflict

Knowing that conflict makes us feel unsafe helps to clarify the initial goals of conflict management: to secure personal safety and to secure scene safety. Once these two goals are secured, the new goal becomes to help those in conflict regain a sense of self-control, which in turn helps them feel safe.

Avoid the desire to resolve a conflict before all parties involved, including you, feel safe. Finding out, "Who started the argument first?" or discussing the particulars of an incident is a conflict resolution goal, not a conflict management goal. While you are securing scene safety, conflicting parties might resolve their differences. For instance, someone might say, "I didn't mean to call Marcy a jerk. I was upset, and I am sorry for blowing off my steam at her. I hope you accept my apology, Marcy." If Marcy trusts the process, she is likely to accept the apology—something she can do only if she feels safe.

If she doesn't accept the apology at that moment, then resolution would have to wait until she and the name caller were willing and able to discuss the dispute without resorting to mean-spirited name-calling.

The operative word of conflict management is safety. Learning to ask "Am I safe?" is the first step before fully engaging in a conflict. Making the scene safe is the second goal of conflict management. These two initial steps help to keep you on task. When safety concerns are addressed, conflict becomes approachable and thus manageable.

Self-Leadership Skills

Creating order from chaos without the use of brute force requires an array of universal conflict management tools. These techniques rely upon your ability to sustain a reasonable amount of self-control and thus self-leadership.

Self-leadership involves making a conscious choice to act in response to conflict. In this context, to act is defined as responding to a conflict without being pulled in emotionally and to remain calm and clearheaded. The use of breathing techniques for maintaining self-control is of the utmost importance. In essence, self-leadership entails choosing to look beyond your self-interest. In the words of Morihei Ueshiba, the founder of Aikido, "True victory is self victory." Changing your approach to conflict is a demanding transformation. The ability to view conflict as neither good nor evil permits you to see through the emotions of the moment and lead conflict out of chaos and toward safety.

To Prevent

Difficulties are meant to rouse, not discourage. The human spirit is to grow strong by conflict.

— William Ellery Channing

The first type of crisis I learned to respond to was a medical emergency. Early on in undergraduate school, I took a First Responders course and, in my senior year, I became certified as an emergency medical technician (EMT). Over the years, I have noticed how EMT skills overlap with those of a conflict-crisis intervener.

The Feel, Look, Listen Approach

In basic first aid, "Look, Listen, and Feel" is part of every initial assessment. Using these same cues, in the order Feel, Look, and Listen, you can learn to observe indicators of potential conflict. The Feel, Look, and Listen Approach to identifying warning indicators is quick and easy to use. From this starting point, indicators that would normally go unnoticed are instead brought to light. Recognizing indicators of an imminent conflict is an essential crisis prevention and conflict management skill.

The following illustration depicts the initial stage of crisis prevention.

CRISIS PREVENTION GOAL	⟶	Keep the Scene Safe by Identifying Potentially Dangerous Indicators Feel, Look, Listen Approach

To feel, in this case, implies paying attention to your gut feeling or intuition.

"Mary seemed off to me yesterday. She just wasn't her old self."

"I had a feeling the students were planning something, but I just didn't listen to myself."

Intuition is the subconscious picking up cues. When you have a gut feeling, pay attention to what your body is telling you. If the hairs on the back of your neck start to rise or your stomach is unusually tight and you find yourself in a defensive posture, then your body may be telling you that there is more than meets the eye, and it would be best to be on guard.

Parents quickly hone this skill. For instance, a mother or father could be talking to a friend one moment and then intuitively turn to catch a child who is falling down. "I just sense when something is going to happen to my son."

Conflict is like a tropical storm. You never really know where or when it is going to touch down. Yet, just as we can feel the atmospheric change in the air of an oncoming storm, we are capable of sensing panic or tension in others.

To look means visually collecting indicators that are threatening or out of place. How are people posturing themselves? Are they in a defensive position? Do they look scared? When there is a large group of people involved, observe the entire group. Making eye contact with the group at large ensures that you are aware of everyone present, even those who are seemingly uninvolved. In doing so, you offer reassurance that you are aware and in charge. You might notice sub-grouping, during which people are moving away from agitators, or the group may be unusually quiet and looking away from potential conflict.

Noticing eyes, hands, posture, and feet can help you detect subtleties about what a person is thinking or feeling. Flaring nostrils occur with fear, anger, and frustration. Clenched fists held tightly at the side are indicators of frustration and anxiety. A squared-off stance with the feet shoulder width apart may be an indicator of preparedness or intimidation. Shifting feet, pacing, and stomping are often indicators of frustration.

Observing body posturing helps to identify additional cues. When a person's arms are held straight at his sides, his chest is puffed outward, and he is standing tall, be cautious. Such a stance is often an indication of readiness for a verbal or physical assault.

To listen means staying alert to all the background noise and up-front discussion taking place around you at the time of an intervention. Is it unusually loud or quiet? What tone of voice is being used? Is it sharp or threatening, or conciliatory? What is really being said? Are you hearing a lively game of cards being played, or is the joking actually antagonistic or at the expense of someone's well-being?

Integrate the Feel, Look, Listen Approach

Incorporating another tool into your conflict management style does take a bit of practice. Initially view the approach as a one, two, and three step process. In time the three components will occur concurrently. For example, feel the mood of the room while looking and listening to the way people involved in conflict are interacting.

The Feel, Look, Listen Approach as a crisis prevention technique encourages us to pay attention to warning indicators.

Breathing as an Indicator

In medical emergencies, first responders feel for a pulse and a patient's breath. In emotional emergencies, the breath is also an important indicator of distress and potential escalation.

Too often the way in which a person (or people) in crisis is or isn't breathing is ignored. Breath is a subtle and powerful indicator of a person's state of well-being. It takes only a bit of practice to learn to observe breathing patterns for signs of agitation, frustration, stress, and fear.

For instance,

1. An agitated person will have flared nostrils and will breathe with force.
2. Heavy sighs or the irritated sounding "psst" as air is blown through the lips are noticeable indicators of frustration and stress.
3. Withheld and shallow breathing are indicators of fear.

Learning to assess breathing patterns and their associated behaviors is an essential conflict management skill. The chapter in this book entitled "Don't Forget to Breathe" will detail further how we breathe and its impact on interveners and people in crisis.

When Indicators are Overlooked

Precautionary measures are taken daily to deter crises in all types of settings. Teachers meet with students and parents to discuss obstacles hindering students' scholastic performance. In residential care settings, staff members mediate disagreements between clients before they escalate into full-blown crises. In acute care facilities where patients are already in crisis, staff members work one-on-one with patients. Human resource departments in the public and private sectors often provide employees the opportunity to take classes in stress reduction and conflict mediation.

Even with the use of precautionary measures, though, conflicts still occur. The outcome can be catastrophic.

***March 6, 2001* – Santee School Shooting**

Fifteen–year–old Andy Williams shot and killed two people and wounded thirteen at his high school in Santee, California, on March 6, 2001. A month prior to the shooting, Andy had been telling his friends that he was going to take his father's gun and bring it to the school to shoot people. His friends later said that they thought he was joking and didn't take him seriously.

Andy had been at the home of his best friend, Josh Stevens. On March 5, 2001, Chris Reynolds, Josh's mom's boyfriend, asked Andy about the threats. Reynolds stated that he had tried calling Andy's father to tell him about Andy's threat to take a weapon to school, but he failed to follow through after getting no answer on the Williams' phone.

December 26, 2000 – Edgewater Shooting

Forty-two-year-old Michael McDermott, a software engineer at Edgewater Technology in Wakefield, Massachusetts, killed seven people on December 26, 2000. After entering his work site, he proceeded to methodically hunt down and shoot seven employees of the e–based firm.

McDermott had been experiencing increasing stress. Earlier that day, he had learned that his vehicle was being repossessed. Edgewater was also about to garnish his wages to pay back taxes he owed the IRS. Like many potential and actual workplace avengers, he had telltale signs of impending volatility, but no one forecast the tragedy.

March, 1998 – State of Connecticut Lottery Shooting

A Connecticut State Lottery employee executed four managers including the executive director in early March 1998 then killed himself after returning from a stress reduction workshop. Coworkers noted in retrospect that he had seemed withdrawn and had never gotten over his disputes with management.

Also in March 1998, thirteen-year-old and eleven-year-old boys shot and killed five people at an Arkansas elementary school. A classmate of the thirteen-year-old recounted a conversation with the boy the day before: "Tomorrow you all find out if you live or die."

"And I said, 'What's that supposed to mean?' And he said ['You'll] find out tomorrow.'"

Why are Indicators Overlooked?

Incidents like those described above leave us in despair. The question arises, "What could have been done to prevent such tragedy?" The obvious answer is to pay attention to even the most subtle of indicators.

Odd comments or abrupt changes in behavior should not go unnoticed. Two weeks before the Arkansas ambush, the thirteen-year-old who had been an avid churchgoer suddenly stopped attending services at church.

Being alert and always on the lookout for danger is challenging. Unless it is part of your job, like a lifeguard or a patrolman who is constantly vigilant and on the lookout for warning indicators, some signs will slip through the cracks. Then again, even when potentially dangerous indicators are noticed, many people do not always know what to do and thus do nothing. A lack of confidence coupled with inadequate training deters would-be interveners. Whether or not you have enough time to intervene is also a factor.

The following two scenarios illustrate what happens when indicators are noted, but interveners don't respond to the signals.

Overwhelmed in the Classroom

As a student teacher, Barbara felt overwhelmed by the responsibilities of managing classroom behaviors of seventh graders. She had enough trouble trying to organize her lesson plan. Therefore, when she overheard a group of boys in her class teasing one of the girls, she figured another, more seasoned teacher would take notice and know how to stop the behavior. Barbara's classroom supervisor, however, did not step in and take charge of the boy's behavior since she expected Barbara to do so or ask for assistance. The girl being teased finally became exasperated and ended up punching one of the boys in the nose.

Passing the Buck

It was two forty-five when Felicia looked at her watch at the emergency shelter for pregnant teens. Only fifteen minutes more until she would be off duty. She knew there was tension between two of the young women who were sitting in the social room. If she could just keep things quiet till three o'clock, the responsibility would fall to someone else to take care of their conflict.

Felicia scooted out of work at three o'clock sharp. When Judy, the second shift worker, came on duty, she had to spend two hours de-escalating the conflict between the two women that Felicia had avoided.

Unfortunately, the two preceding scenarios are all too common and highlight the following—

- Being overwhelmed fosters incompetence.
- Being unskilled puts those who are in your care at risk.
- Putting self-interest ahead of others, much like Felicia did, undermines the success of the work site.

Content as an Obstacle

Not all people lack the time needed to intervene. Many people have basic skills in conflict management. And, thankfully, human service workers often do put their own self-interest aside to help others. So why, then, do capable people still allow conflicts to get the better of them both in their personal lives and at work?

Our ability to make sense of an incident is often compromised by our emotions. Put more simply—we get caught up in the content of the conflict.

The story line of a conflict, what I call the content, is the

"Who done it?"

" What happened?"

and often the

"Who is to blame?"

Each question is important, if you are a police detective. For the rest of us, getting into the content too quickly is unproductive at best and dangerous at the worst. Take my advice and "drop the content." Not only will you avoid making a mountain out of a mole-hill next time you intervene during a crisis, but you can also use it as a preventive measure to manage reoccurring conflicts.

Dropping the Content During an Intervention

If you were to ask two people who were arguing, "What happened?" or "Who started it?" what would each person do at the same time?

Or imagine this—

You are having an argument and someone neutral comes up to the two of you and offers her assistance with any one of the typical questions:

"What's the problem?"

"Can I help?"

"What's going on?"

I'm not sure about you, but if it happened to me, and I was even slightly emotionally charged, I would defend my point of view. And, there is a very high probability that the person who I was arguing with would do the same thing, too.

I know we ask content questions with the intention of wanting to help solve the problem. Content Seeking Interveners (CSI) think that by finding out what started the fight or what the current disagreement is all about will somehow enable them to right a wrong. Right?

Wrong? Not only does getting into the content at this stage of the game further incite the conflict, it also makes the two parties feel even less successful. Avoiding the content until all parties have had time to regain a semblance of self-control will help provide a win\win outcome.

Arguments can go from zero to sixty in no time at all. Resolving the same argument can take years, days, hours, or sometime it never gets resolved at all. Ask yourself, when was the last time you fully resolved a conflict. Resolution means fini, complete, done. It is a good goal to have, but an unrealistic one to undertake when tempers are flaring.

Before we get into how "dropping the content" can be used in the crisis prevention technique, the following scenarios will further help define the technique of dropping the content during an intervention.

Breaking Through a Mother's Lament

Mary was putting her last load of laundry in the washer when she heard a loud crash. She rushed up from the basement to the first floor and found her three kids—Johnny, four, Jimmy, six, and Joey, eight—staring wide-eyed at broken glass on the kitchen floor. Mary saw the boys' football on the floor next to her late grandmother's now broken teapot.

"How many times have I told you boys to keep that football outside?" screamed Mary. "I told your father not to play with you indoors. Oh, God! My mother told me not to leave my good china out where you kids could get to it. Why couldn't I have had three girls instead of boys? Wait till your father gets back from the store." Luke, Mary's husband, happened to hear Mary's last statement as he walked in through the front door. "What about me?" he called out.

"Luke, I told you not to play with the boys inside. Look what they have done this time. I have been working all morning just so we could go out to the fair this afternoon. This is the thanks I get for working so hard." Mary turned and stomped off to her bedroom and said in a low, clear voice, "Damn you all."

After Luke directed his sons to clean up the mess, he went to the bedroom door and knocked. "May I come in?" asked Luke.

He heard a small, whispered, "Yes," and entered.

"Feel like talking?"

"I'm so mad."

"Say more."

"I'm mad at everyone—you, the kids, my mother." Mary let out a small laugh. "God. I can't believe myself sometimes. Where did all that stuff come from? That little teapot was so special to me, Luke. I used to sit with my grandmother drinking tea, and we would both pretend that we were princesses. Isn't that silly?"

"Sounds pretty sweet to me."

"I just lost myself when I saw that it was broken. I feel stupid for not taking my mother's advice."

"No blaming, okay?"

"I feel like I lost a piece of myself when I saw the glass on the floor."

Luke actively listened to Mary. The skill of active listening utilizes leading statements that engage the speaker. For example, "Could you say more?" or "Please go on." Active listening may also be nonverbal, as when you nod or shake your head, signifying understanding and interest. Because of Luke's active listening and feedback, Mary was able to gain clarity and change her focus from being angry to speaking about the loss of her teapot. If Mary had been unable or unwilling to participate in this conversation, she might have spent the rest of the day in her bedroom sulking.

Learning to drop the content, the "Who done it?" or the "Who is to blame?" can help identify the root of one's emotional outburst. In Mary's case, she realized that seeing her broken teapot caused her anguish. By actively listening,

Luke helped her to drop the content. Dropping the content as a preventive measure helps to reveal harmful behaviors. Being explosive and lashing out, as Mary did, serves no one. After dropping the content, she was able to reflect upon her behavior and find a less destructive response, while still acknowledging her feelings.

Regretting the incident after she was able to drop the content, Mary might say, "I can't believe what I said to the kids, Luke. I told them that I wished I had girls, instead of boys. What was I thinking? My anger got the best of me. If I had told them how sad I was to see the teapot was broken, I know they would be more careful next time. Instead they only saw me at my worst. I don't like them saying mean things to each other. I have to try not to do the same thing myself."

Dropping the content can be done by yourself or with the help of another person. For instance, sometimes I say drop the content to myself. By mentally stepping back from the scene that is unfolding, I am often able to remain non-reactive and cut to the source of potential conflict. Instead of a sterile response to the situation or a reactive response, I find that my objective self is able to make a better connection with those involved than when I allow my emotions to guide me. Clarity is a powerful perspective that draws in those who lack stability.

In Aikido I train to project a non-reactive posture. I stand with my hands down along my sides and my feet slightly offset so that one foot is forward. My knees stay flexed, and I usually have a smile on my face, not a grimace. This stance looks completely non-threatening. In effect, I drop the content of potential conflict by standing in an open posture, eliciting dialogue. It can disarm an attacker when the object of the attack stands in an open posture that exudes confidence and clarity.

Thus, Aikido teaches a way to drop the physical content of a conflict that may be displayed through body language. Active listening is a similar technique that can create a way to drop the content in a conflict. The following is a glimpse of two different conversations where content is an obstacle and active listening helps to drop the content.

Unveiling a Holiday Drama

"When my sister walked into the room, I felt my forehead begin to sweat," Christopher told his housemate, Lisa. "I couldn't believe she was there! And she brought her new boyfriend! She is always waltzing in with someone new, like she owns the whole world. All she ever gives my family is this one little three-hour blast at Christmas. My parents rag on me every time she leaves. I'm always left picking up all the pieces for her, trying to settle down my mother and father, who keep asking me where they went wrong."

Once Christopher quieted down, Lisa asked him if he wanted to say more about his sister.

"I don't know. I just feel so upset by it all."

"What's the real issue here, Chris?" Lisa asked.

"This stuff between us is so old. Things are never gonna change between her and me."

In the exchange, Lisa encouraged Chris to drop the content.

Chris asked, "What do you mean?"

"Being with family can kick up a lot of old feelings. You get a kind of snowball effect. Everything is all mushed together. Squeeze out the essentials." Lisa explained.

"Meaning what?" asked Chris.

"Meaning," Lisa went on, "start at the beginning. You said your forehead began to sweat when your sister walked into the room. Was that because she had a new boyfriend or because you were worrying about your folks, or what?"

Chris made a small, sad laugh and said, "I just miss her. I miss my sister! She was the one I depended on."

Dropping the content takes courage because conflict impacts us on an emotional level. It would have been easier for Chris to continue to gripe about his sister than to be vulnerable by admitting that he missed her. Venting requires no individual responsibility for your part in a conflict, and you can complain about another person or group until the sun sets tomorrow. Dropping the content, however, does require self-assessment and the ability to accept responsibility for your own role in a conflict.

Instead of judging his sister's actions by saying or thinking, "She is always waltzing in with someone new, like she owns the whole world," dropping the content for Chris required him to assess his own actions about his sister: "I just miss her. I miss my sister!" Perhaps next time he saw his sister, he could avoid getting mad and instead try a different tack that might include a request to renew their friendship or simply tell her, "I miss you."

A Couple's Quarrel

As soon as Nicole got into her best friend Maria's car, she began to recount her recent saga with Tony. "I know I told him that my mother was visiting, you see, but he doesn't listen to me. So the next thing I know, he is stomping around upstairs making my life miserable. He's all upset because she was still there and supposedly we were expected for dinner at our friend's, Pete and Sue's. How would I know that he made plans for us to go out? He acts like a baby. I can't stand it. We hardly spoke to each other for the rest of the evening!"

"Wow," Maria said. "You guys aren't getting along."

Nicole replied, "What do you think I'm trying to tell you? Isn't it obvious? He just doesn't include me in on anything. I'm supposed to be his wife, but I feel more like a slave."

Although venting about a conflict can be healthy, it has a tendency to be destructive, like Mary's outburst over the teapot. Redirecting Nicole away from this path could help her to prevent conflict with Tony from escalating or recurring.

"Is this about your mom?" inquired Maria.

"I wish it was that easy," said Nicole.

"Is it about Pete and Sue?"

"No. I love those guys. And we did go over once my mom left."

"So, what do you think this argument was about?" encouraged Maria.

"All our arguments are about the same thing. He doesn't talk to me. And I don't talk to him. I guess we never really took time to talk, even when we first got together," said Nicole in a sad and quiet tone.

In this last statement, Nicole identified a key point of her distress: "He doesn't talk to me. And I don't talk to him." Their inability to communicate will likely continue to impact their lives. Revealing a harmful pattern is a first step in finding a solution and preventing the behavior from recurring. Nicole could seek individual counseling for improving her own communication skills, but it is likely that she would want her husband to make a commitment to work on his skills, too. If Nicole said to Tony, "We have lousy communication skills," Tony would likely become defensive and disagree: "I don't know what you are talking about. I communicate just fine." Like Chris, Nicole should have stated her role and let Tony take responsibility for himself: "Tony, I would like to work on the way I communicate with you. I am not sure how to do this. I am going to need your help. Would you be willing to set aside some time this week after dinner to help me out?" Tony could then decide his part in Nicole's attempt to better their relationship.

Dropping the Content a Preventive and Intervention Tool

As a preventive measure for repetitive behavior and as an intervention tool, dropping the content can be used in two ways as demonstrated in the following vignettes. Although these may appear very site-specific, the same scenario with a different cast of characters can be found in many homes and work sites.

Steve's Socks

Every Wednesday, like clockwork, at the adult mental health residential treatment center, Steve has an explosive outburst when he finishes his laundry. He says, "Who took my T-shirt?" or "Hey! One of my socks is missing!" Steve has been known to go barging into other resident's rooms, slinging profanities, and demanding to check their dresser drawers.

Staff and residents alike were fed up with his behavior. "We have tried everything: marking his clothes, giving him a special basket for his laundry, and even staying with him while he washes his clothes. Nothing seems to work."

The effort had focused solely on keeping Steve's clothes intact. Without dropping the content, everyone was overlooking a harmful behavior, which was how Steve handled his anger. Steve might never be happy with his clothes, so that wasn't the real point. One day he might find that he has all his articles but a sweater shrank or colors ran, and his temper would erupt again.

Exposing a harmful behavior, like Steve's unbridled anger, is a starting point. In all likelihood, the same behavior would arise again. Additional guidance would be required to help remind him how to manage his anger.

Sheryl's Work Site Behavior

Sheryl was a fast, articulate talker. She was also known as an antagonist and was typically found in the middle of conflicts, either egging on two other parties or intimidating someone else.

Mrs. Lewis had just been told that Sheryl was being transferred to her department at Community Insurance Incorporated. She was also told that Sheryl rambled on and on when she was angry and had difficulty listening to anyone until she had settled down. Once she had controlled her anger, however, she was a good listener and one of CII's best workers. Mrs. Lewis was scheduled to meet with her to discuss her new job duties.

When someone hears statements like "Sheryl is a manipulator and could talk her way out of a bag," it is hard not to pass judgment. The tendency is to discuss the behavior and not the precipitant of the behavior. If Mrs. Lewis were to begin their meeting discussing Sheryl's behavior, Sheryl would surely take the defensive.

Sheryl, like Steve, needed to learn how to manage anger. Mrs. Lewis could use the qualities needed for her new job placement as the vehicle for discussing Sheryl's communication and anger management skills. Learning to manage harmful behavior helps those in perpetual conflict understand potential obstacles to their success.

Starting a Dialogue with Sheryl

Once they had gone through the basic introductory hellos, Mrs. Lewis began by saying, "Sheryl, we are meeting this morning to speak about your new duties here at CII. You are a skilled worker, and this position will be an exciting new challenge. What were you hoping to bring to this new team?"

"I am a good listener and love to work hard on new ideas," said Sheryl.

"Could you say more about your attributes as a good listener?" inquired Mrs. Lewis. "I am expecting you to be a leader, and I know that role can have its ups and downs."

Mrs. Lewis left the door open for Sheryl to begin discussing her strengths. She also directed the conversation toward communication skills and the dynamics of a team, instead of confronting Sheryl by saying, "I know you have a hard time working with others." Mrs. Lewis put Sheryl in the driver's seat. "Could you say more?" was an enticing request that allowed Sheryl to reflect upon her work style and communication skills.

Recurring Conflict Due to Repetitive Behavior

Many everyday behaviors, like squabbling with others or failing to communicate needs in a non-confrontational manner, can't be changed overnight, and certainly won't be changed by merely demanding that a person "shape up or ship out." Bear in mind that most people are doing the best they can with the tools they have. Until you are guided toward another way to respond to a difficult situation, you will keep going back to what is most familiar.

Repetitive Behavior has two levels of understanding.

- Level 1 Repetitive Behavior is defined as the most obvious behavior.
- Level 2 Repetitive Behavior is defined as the underlying cause driving the most obvious behavior.

The following list highlights common examples of Level 1 Repetitive Behavior (L1) and Level 2 Repetitive Behavior (L2). Please note that the L2 can be a myriad of behaviors. Suffice it to say that L2 can be a psychosis. These behaviors can be found in many different settings.

- L1 – A family member who always disrupts a dinner.

  Possible L2:

  May have difficulty sitting still.
- L1 – A client who continually disrupts group meetings.

Possible L2s:

Believes that negative attention is the correct way to get help.

Has no concept of respectful boundaries for others.

- L1 – A son who abuses car privileges by leaving the tank empty after each use

  Possible L2:

  No one in the family respects individual property and privacy.

- L1 – A resident at a treatment facility who abuses telephone privileges by staying on the line longer than the time allocated.

  Possible L2:

  Has always gotten very caught up in the moment and is not very good at letting go or self-monitoring

- L1 – A student who disrupts the class everyday by distracting other students.

  Possible L2:

  Has no concept of waiting to speak or respecting others' boundaries and personal space.

- L1 – A patient who constantly demands to have her medication or cigarettes

  Possible L2:

  Has a learned behavior that the loudest or most demanding person gets attention.

  Is scared of being forgotten.

- L1 – A student who regularly fights during recess.

  Possible L2s:

  Has been bullied.

  Has been encouraged to bully.

- L1 – An employee who is always late or calling in sick for work.

  Possible L2s:

  Time management difficulties

  Depression

L2 Repetitive Behavior is often masked by the more outrageous L1 Repetitive Behavior. Until one's behavior is changed or redirected, conflict will continue, often with increasing intensity.

Creating an Action Plan

Creating an action plan for repetitive behavior prevents conflicts from recurring. It is a proactive measure to take for those who seek to move beyond the crippling and at times explosive effect of repetitive behavior. For instance, if you find yourself always losing your temper, an action plan can help you manage your anger before it gets explosive.

The time to create an action plan is not when you are in the middle of an argument or going to the activity that repeatedly triggers unwanted behaviors. Think of yourself when you are angry and in conflict. Can you really listen to someone who might have good advice? Likely not. Why?—because you are already thinking about the difficult conversation that you are about to have. The time to work on an action plan is when the person in need is able to listen and commit to a new course of action. If there are conflicting parties needing to work through a conflict, they have to be composed and willing to engage with each other. Learning to take responsibility for our actions is an important life skill.

Timing for a Professional Intervener

So many of the tools we need to manage conflict and help others are already familiar or at the very least similar to jobs we have had in the past. For example, helping a client set up an action plan is, for me, much like helping a group of first time campers have a successful backpacking trip.

If they don't have a good first trip and feel uncomfortable setting up a tent, they will likely never want to sleep in a tent again or consider a hike in the woods. So usually a week or two before going out on the overnight trip, I would make sure all the food was packed and ready. We also practiced setting up our tent at the home base at least once before we headed out. That way the tent would go up effortlessly when we arrived at camp, tired and more in need of food than a first time lesson in tent construction. My overall goal was to make sure that campers went home with happy memories of their first night out in the woods. The same overall approach can be taken when helping to create an action plan.

What's that? You never led a group of kids out on an overnight? Well then, consider every other activity that you have engaged in over the years, from packing for a vacation to getting the car ready for winter travel or the house or windows in your apartment ready for winter winds. Life offers us lots of opportunities to prepare, set up, and instruct others or ourselves on how to use the proper tools and techniques to ensure a rewarding first adventure and avoid an experience in misery.

The following techniques are key to helping create a workable action plan.

Active listening

Demonstrate that you are sincerely
interested in what is being said.

Practice dropping the content.

The solution becomes clear once a
harmful behavior is revealed.

Pay attention to your intuition.

If you get a hunch that the conflict is being fueled
by repetitive behavior, take note.

Timing Your Intervention

Managing repetitive behavior requires timing your intervention so that the person you are trying to help is willing and able to listen.

Let's revisit some of our friends from a few pages back and see how the timing of the intervention impacted them.

- Mary needed a little time alone before she could speak to Luke.
- Christopher needed to emote before he could make sense of his conflict with his sister.
- Nicole needed to talk with someone other than Tony in order to gain clarity on her marriage.
- Mrs. Lewis timed her intervention by slowly moving into the discussion with Sheryl instead of bringing up her behavior as the first subject.

A person in conflict who is hampered by repetitive behavior has to be able and willing to listen to alternatives. It is in no one's best interest to begin such a dialogue when emotions are still highly charged.

What follows is an example of purposeful timing of an intervention in order to make a collaborative action plan for managing a student's behavior.

Recess with Hector

Hector, a fifth grader at Pine Street Elementary School, frequently got into fights with other students at recess. He was given a number of detentions, and teachers had been meeting with his mother without Hector present to discuss his behavior.

During the Monday afternoon teacher's meeting, Ms. Smith, his new homeroom teacher, asked if anyone had discussed with Hector what he could or couldn't hear from a teacher when he was getting upset. "We all have buttons that are easily pushed when someone says just the right word to get us going. I wonder if we are saying the wrong thing to him," Ms. Smith said to the others, and then she volunteered to ask him.

Wednesday afternoon during the detention period, Ms. Smith asked Hector to come up to her desk. "Hector, I need your help tomorrow," she said.

"What do you mean?" asked Hector.

"Well," replied Ms. Smith, "I keep blowing it, saying all the wrong things to you when you are at recess."

"My mom says our whole family has a temper. Don't worry about it," said Hector with a sheepish grin.

"When you are getting upset, is there anything that your mom says or someone else says that helps you think about what you are doing? Come on, Hector, tell me something that will make you smile like you are doing now. I know you want to do the right thing," urged Ms. Smith.

"If you want to say something to me, how about, 'Do the right thing'? I like that," said Hector.

"Okay. Next time during recess, if I see that you are getting upset with a classmate, I'm going to say 'Hector, do the right thing.' When I say that, I would like you to look right at me and nod your head and then take two steps back away from whomever you are talking to. Sounds kind of silly, huh? But I think it might work. Are you willing to try it?" asked Ms. Smith.

Hector agreed to try. The playground disputes decreased after that initial meeting with Hector. Ms. Smith was pleased to hear Hector say, "Do the right thing" whenever he ran by her on his way out to recess.

Identifying recurring behavior and meeting with a person when he or she is willing or able to listen is all part of how you create an action plan. People, regardless of their history, have times when they are receptive to hearing and discussing things in a rational way. Finding that moment takes time and patience, but is well worth the effort.

Let's revisit Steve and see how an action plan could be created to help him manage his anger.

Steve's Action Plan

On Monday, two days before Steve did his laundry, Kevin, a worker at Steve's site, set up a meeting time with Steve for two in the afternoon, a quiet time when the television wasn't on. Steve usually spent his time reading in his room. He was excited about the meeting with Kevin, which he understood was an opportunity to discuss his laundry.

At exactly two o'clock, Steve was outside Kevin's office, knocking to come in. Kevin rose up out of his chair, opened the door for Steve, and greeted him by saying, "Hi, Steve. Please take a seat here next to my desk." Kevin usually just called out, "Come in." Instead, Kevin tried to set a pace that was formal, hoping that Steve would follow his lead and act less frantic and more businesslike.

Steve smiled and took a seat. Kevin said, "I want to begin by thanking you for taking the time to meet with me this afternoon. I know this is your free time. I have some ideas about laundry day that I think might help you."

"Good, good," Steve said. "You have my full attention. I have some thoughts too, like letting me do my laundry first. I'll get up early and get it done before breakfast."

"Wow," Kevin replied. "That is a pretty gracious offer. I am willing to explore that idea."

The two men discussed the morning routine, and Kevin noticed how thoroughly Steve made plans to get up before the rest of the group. He said he would let Steve try doing his laundry early Wednesday morning. They agreed to meet later in the day and review how things went.

Kevin then asked Steve to set up an action plan in case there turned out to be a problem with his laundry that morning. "This action plan is much like what you presented to me, but it is designed to deal with any problems that may occur. I want you to be successful and get your laundry done without any hitches. For instance, what if the machine doesn't work right or the last person using it left it dirty? How would you manage that?"

Kevin noticed Steve's face had tensed up and his face was flushed. "I'm with you, Steve. Keep breathing," Kevin said.

Steve let out a small breath of air and looked down at the floor.

"What you are doing right now may help this Wednesday," Kevin added.

Bewildered, Steve looked up at Kevin.

"Notice how you are breathing and thinking about what I said? That is great. You're taking your time and controlling your emotions. I know you can do that if a problem arises with your laundry."

"I guess," said Steve.

Kevin continued to engage Steve in designing a plan for managing his reaction to problems that might arise when he did his laundry.

Over the next few months, Kevin maintained an atmosphere of appreciation toward Steve for continuing to manage his behavior while directing him to look at obstacles that impeded his success. Taking time to pave a path toward success is a crucial step in the creation of a workable action plan for managing harmful behaviors. First, of course, both parties need to agree about what a successful outcome is. The common goal for Kevin and Steve was to get the laundry done and to manage laundry mishaps, like a lost sock, without Steve becoming explosive.

The next vignette will present you with three options for managing a harmful behavior. Each option is viable, but only one will truly help Jerome manage his repetitive behavior.

Jerome's Phone Call

Every Monday night at the emergency shelter for adolescents, Jerome called his father. Sharon, the second shift supervisor, could set her clock by the moment that Jerome finally got upset at his father's tirade and slammed the receiver down, turning his anger on the other residents in the hallway. Sharon said, "Jerome gets in everybody's face, and once I almost had to call the police to come and assist me when Jerome was refusing to come in off the front lawn one night after a call. He was kicking over the garbage cans in our driveway and cussing. I can't let that type of behavior occur in a residential neighborhood. I also can't prevent him from talking to his dad. I just don't know what to do."

Which Action Plan Is a Good Approach for Jerome?

Jerome – Option 1

Sharon knew that Jerome got mad whenever he talked to his dad on the phone. Sharon found him that night in the social room, about fifteen minutes before he usually made his call, and asked him into the office to discuss other ways to work with the difficult telephone call.

Jerome – Option 2

Sharon told Jerome that he had to call his father on Friday afternoon when fewer residents were in the shelter instead of Monday nights when the shelter was full. Sharon and the rest of the treatment team decided that the next time Jerome had an angry outburst due to his phone calls with his dad, he would be fully reprimanded and come down one point, which could take away his eligibility to go to the movie theater that weekend.

Jerome – Option 3

Sharon decided to talk to Jerome on Friday about his Monday night phone call. On Fridays, Jerome always got back from work fifteen minutes before everyone else, so they would have privacy, and Jerome's confidentiality would be protected. During the meeting, Sharon asked Jerome what happened every time he talked with his dad on Monday nights. "Oh, I don't know, Sharon," Jerome replied. "He always calls me a loser or something."

"What do you do when he calls you a loser?" inquired Sharon.

"You mean the way I get mad?" asked Jerome. Sharon nodded and Jerome went on, "Well, I can't stand it when he gets on my case, so I just hang up."

Sharon and Jerome then discussed what to do when he got fed up listening to his dad. They worked through a role play of Jerome talking on the phone with his dad and agreed to meet at least fifteen minutes before the phone call on Monday to reaffirm their new strategy.

The goal of creating an action plan is to find a way that will help the other person be successful. The real issue is teaching Jerome to manage his anger, not whether he calls his father on Friday or Monday. Sharon might be able to give some guidance over the long term in relation to his father, but in the short term, her goal is to help Jerome learn how to manage his anger. Therefore, Option 3 is the strategy with the most potential to help Jerome.

The next illustration outlines the completion of the crisis prevention goal by creating an action plan after dropping the content.

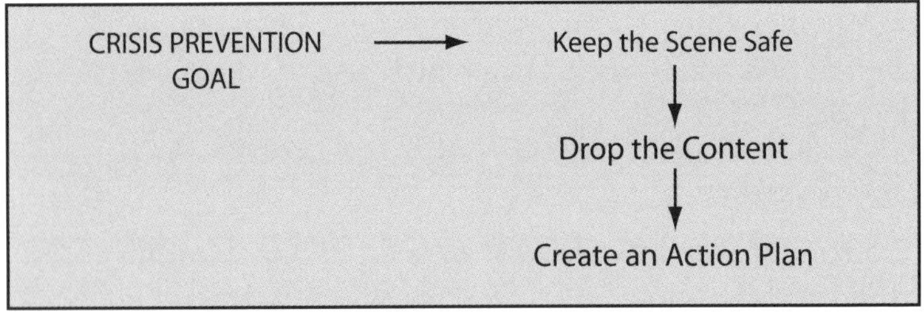

Summary: Living Is Hard Work

Meeting day-to-day needs of food and shelter is only the tip of the iceberg in terms of what each of us needs to survive if we are to actively engage in life. If you're not living off the land in total isolation, you are going to need communication skills, and getting along with others is not always going to be trouble-free. Conflict happens. The important thing to remember is that you are able to have an impact on how conflict affects your life.

The Feel, Look, Listen Approach is an accessible technique for observing potentially dangerous indicators. It provides a vantage point for observing escalating behavior. Being prepared for conflict feels a whole lot better than being paranoid and consumed by the fear of impending conflict.

Removing the melodrama associated with so many conflicts is also a skill that requires observation and active listening. Dropping the content removes drama and helps reveal harmful behaviors that can become repetitive and contribute to recurring or escalating conflicts.

One of the best investments in conflict prevention is having an action plan that helps manage potential crisis or harmful behaviors. You can create workable action plans. Begin with small increments of success, ensuring a strong foundation. Avoid making action plans that are too complex.

There will be conflicts and crises that come on unexpectedly. Your preparedness for handling everyday squabbles and mini-crises will come in handy during such times. In Aikido, we practice a single technique over and over. Practice, practice, practice is the mantra of all students who want to master an art. As I go over and over the same technique, I find that by going slower or speeding up, subtle changes occur to my physical and emotional balance. The depth of learning is never-ending. New students to Aikido can become impatient with the repetition of practicing the same technique over and over. In time they soon learn that many techniques are lovingly called "a thirty-year technique" or a "twenty-year technique." meaning that it takes at the minimum 30 or 20 years to perfect a single movement.

In my private life, I have often found myself getting stuck in the same argument with the same person over the same topic. Like the new Aikido student, I can feel impatient, wanting the conflict to go away so I can move on. If Aikido has thirty-year techniques, then those personal conflicts that trouble me most are likely sixty-year-old techniques. Yep, that sure is a long time to get it right.

My mom taught me a saying when I was fourteen that has helped me keep such life lessons in perspective. "Don't let your highs get too high or your lows get too low." There will be obstacles that each of us has to face during our lives, and conflict will be a constant. In order to manage my own anger, I keep my mom's saying in the back of my mind and realize that seeking balance in life takes hard work, compassion, preparedness, and practice.

Am I Safe?

If you cry "Forward," you must make plain in what direction to go.

— Anton Chekov

Early on in my career I used to say, "Every situation is different. There is no one set recipe for intervening." Back then I would teach a range of skills from paraphrasing to body posturing. I figured the more options the better. To say I have eaten those words a thousand times since would be an understatement.

My turn around in viewpoint occurred for me while facilitating yet one more role play during a seminar. I noticed that everyone, no matter how skilled they were, all kept getting stuck at the same moment of the intervention. For the most part, the scenes I watch are fictional, meaning they are role plays of what an actual argument might be like in the real world. Role-playing how to address angry people is time well spent, considering that we all encounter conflict.

I noticed two consistent trouble spots for people role-playing the "intervener." First, they said too much during their intervention. Saying too much overwhelms the person you are trying to help. Consider this—Have you ever been "drunk on your own rage"? It would be a rare person who hasn't experienced a moment of inner rage. The ability to hear what others are saying to us is compromised when we are angry. A person who is intoxicated can only hear one or two words spoken to them at a time. Once they sober up, they usually can't remember the conversation. Rage, like alcohol, is intoxicating and like alcohol, it can blur our vision and impair our hearing. When speaking to someone who is "drunk on his own rage," the less you say the more likely you will be heard.

Secondly, role-playing "interveners" had no idea of how to manage the conflict at hand, except that they wanted "it," the conflict, to stop. At this moment during the role play, we would hear, "I don't know what to do." Being frightened by the scene unfolding before you conjures up all types of internal dialogues such as, "Why me?" "How did this start?" or "Why didn't I see it coming?" Pertinent as such questions may be, they can rarely be answered during an intervention. The important question for the intervener is, "What is my goal?"

Debunking the "Que Sera, Sera" Conflict Management Style

It became clear that interveners always entered by asking "What's the problem?" or "What happened?" As mentioned in the previous chapter, interveners failed to drop the content. When I see a role player looking bewildered, stuck in the content, and unable to manage a conflict, I ask, "What is your goal?" The range of responses varies from "What do you mean?" to "My goal is to stop the conflict."

Perhaps with brute force you could physically stop another person from pummeling someone else. An authority figure like a parent or police officer could demand that someone stops his or her actions. For the most part, though, when brute force is used, the end result is that someone gets hurt. When I ask the role player how they expect to stop the conflict besides using brute force, there is often no set plan. In other words they are winging it. Making it through by the seat of your pants is neither safe nor effective. Would you want a fire department or paramedic responding haphazardly to your needs? Imagine a burning house and people dangling out of the window. If the firefighters arrived and never had a drill on how to use the water hose or ladder, precious time would be lost as they figured out how to turn the water on and put up the ladder.

It would be ridiculous for a paramedic to ask a choking person "What were you eating?" before helping her dislodge the obstruction. A choking person can barely breathe, never mind talk. Instead of winging it, firefighters and paramedics do practice drills. When a real emergency does occur, they know exactly what to do, and they all have the same goal—to make sure that they are safe so they can create safety for all.

I found that I could use the same main ingredient of "safety first" that first responders use, and incorporate it into a Goal-Oriented Intervention. This new approach to conflict management has a set protocol for interveners to follow that, though similar to emergency first aid, is indeed tailored specifically for emotional emergencies.

Instead of trying to solve the crisis or find out the particulars of the events that lead up to the crisis, interveners keep their sights on securing safety first. Securing safety for a firefighter means putting out the fire, getting people out the house, and keeping spectators at bay. Safety for a paramedic means stabilizing the patient and transporting him to the hospital. Safety for a crisis intervener is broken down into two stages: personal safety and scene safety. Like firefighters, crisis interveners need to insure for their own personal safety so they can help others. When you feel personally safe from harm, you're able to think clearly and remain emotionally unaffected by angry words directed at you. You are also likely to exhaust your breadth of verbal responses before resorting to a physical response.

With personal safety secured, you then move onto helping others or what first responders call stabilizing the patient. I call this step "Scene Safety." With scene safety, you take into account the people or person in crisis; spectators; and physical factors such as furniture, exit routes, and tight quarters that can hinder management of a conflict. The next chapter, entitled "Is the Scene Safe?" will detail scene safety.

The following vignette is an illustration of what can happen when interveners try to stop a conflict before securing personal safety

Mr. Smith Forsakes Personal Safety

> *It was the second-class period of the day at City High. Mr. Smith was taking his turn to check the bathrooms for kids trying to sneak a smoke. As he approached the door, he could hear muffled voices in what sounded like an argument. His palms felt sweaty, and his pulse quickened as he flung the doors open and walked into the bathroom. "All I remember are the lights going out and something hitting me hard on my head," said Mr. Smith after he was rescued. "After that, I just blacked out."*

A drug transaction had been going on in the bathroom when Mr. Smith entered. He hadn't thought twice about his own safety. The following vignette replays Mr. Smith's intervention, but this time with him paying close attention to his personal safety.

Mr. Smith Asks "Am I Safe?"

> *It was the second-class period of the day at City High, and Mr. Smith was taking his turn to check the bathroom for kids trying to sneak a smoke. As he approached the door, he heard muffled voices that sounded like an argument. He took a moment to listen outside the door and asked himself "Am I safe?" He then slowed himself down, since he noticed his palms were sweaty and his heart was pounding. Determining that it was indeed an argument, Mr. Smith waved to Mr. Dempsey, a teacher who was monitoring the hall. He put his hands together to form a T and mouthed the word "trouble."*
>
> *Mr. Dempsey nodded his head that he understood, grabbed the phone inside his room, and called the main office. Mr. Dempsey then came closer to the bathroom. Mr. Smith opened the door with his foot and yelled into the bathroom, "Come on out in the hall, boys! Now!"*

Pausing outside the bathroom door and evaluating the level of risk kept Mr. Smith from rushing in and trying to intervene in a scene that was unsafe. Confined and crowded space, such as a bathroom with multiple hiding places for would-be attackers, requires a team approach. Even with additional teachers, the police might need to be called. Most crisis intervention trainings for teachers do not teach advanced physical management skills, such as escorting a person out of a confined space that could turn into a riot scene. Remember, it takes only a small crowd to create disorder.

Managing multiple would-be attackers requires advanced skills in physical management. Most teachers are authorized to use only two-person escorts, which means each teacher is holding one of the student's arms. When a room is filled with highly agitated people and you have only two interveners responding, it is not realistic to think that you can hold one person safely and expect the rest of the group to stand by, unless you are a police officer. A uniformed police officer projects authority, yet even police officers must still be cautious, though they are granted more authority than the average citizen or teacher.

Be cautious of the I-can-take-care-of-myself attitude. There is always risk of injury involved when a conflict requires hands-on interventions. Calculate the potential dangers of a situation before entering a scene alone. Investigating criminal activity is best left to qualified professionals in law enforcement. If you are expected to catch a person in the act of committing a crime, however, you should have the proper training for such high-risk situations. Waiting for the students to come out of the bathroom on their own accord reduces the overall risk of harm for both the teachers and the students.

Self-control

Assessing your own level of self-control is the first step when you are working toward personal safety. Dick Guere, a friend and teacher who worked in a prison, taught me the following: "If you are not in control of yourself, you are destined to be controlled by others." The loss of control can be physical, mental, or emotional. Whether it is one or all three at the same time matters not. Any way you slice it, the end result is that you are not at your full potential.

It is easy to say, "Get a grip on yourself!" or "You have got to get control of yourself," but what does that really mean? Self-control is the ability to exercise restraint over your own impulses, emotions, or desires. Cultivating self-control is critical when ascertaining personal safety. When making a Goal-Oriented Intervention, the first question asked is "Am I safe?" as Mr. Smith did in the previous vignette.

Am I Safe?

Although your first reaction may be to run directly into a room where two people are arguing, it is not the safest choice, as demonstrated by Mr. Smith, nor the most effective. Thus before entering a conflict as an intervener, the first question to ask is "Am I safe?" It is a simple question—although it might seem rhetorical or foolish, it is very important. Certainly firefighters, police officers, and emergency personnel consider it worthwhile. So why not give it a try?

The following illustration shows what to do after asking, "Am I safe?"

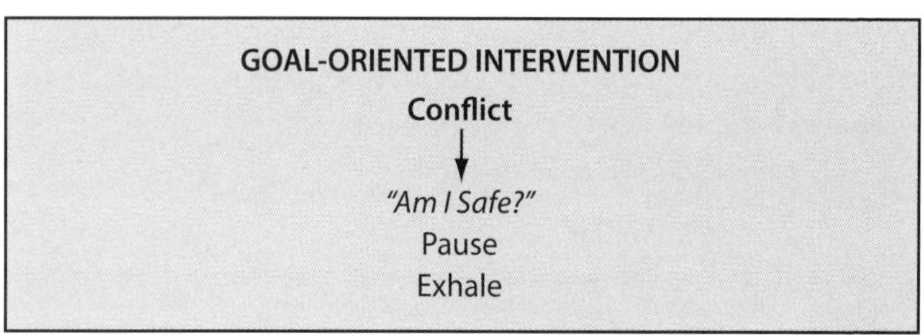

Pause

The pause and exhale are two techniques that are done during the initial stage of intervention. A pause can take up to five seconds and is done simply by stopping yourself before entering the scene of a conflict. For example, after entering a room where you hear loud and angry voices, you would stand just inside the doorway for a moment without speaking. The pause provides you with an opportunity to gauge your own level of self-control. The pause can have a calming effect on those observing by projecting that you are in charge of yourself. After all, when you are the intervener, nothing is worse than being agitated and flustered.

Pausing before engaging in a conflict is a subtle, yet powerful, technique, showing that the intervener is comfortable with both her role and the silence of the moment. A silent moment can feel awkward if constant interaction is the norm, but it is nevertheless effective. Before practicing for the first time with an angry person, try it during a casual conversation. Simply stand quietly inside the doorway upon entering a room, and notice how heads will turn.

Exhale

A slow and deliberate exhale is done simultaneously with the pause. Exhaling is a kick-start for the respiratory system to supply oxygen to the brain. When we are agitated or fearful, we tend to hold our breath or take only short, shallow breaths. When we are intervening, both the quality and quantity of breath taken can impact critical decision-making. The brain needs oxygen for clear thinking. Deep and deliberate breathing helps us to remain calm and clearheaded.

When I first started teaching courses in crisis intervention, I would say, “Remember to breathe.” I found over time, though, that most people inhale first when they think, “Breathe.” Inhaling during a critical event like a conflict does not necessarily mean you will automatically exhale. As long as your body has oxygen, your reflex to exhale may be delayed for a moment. You could continue to hold your breath for quite a long time, even while speaking. Holding your breath is not quality breathing. Your lungs would prefer to have a fresh and consistent supply of oxygen. Ideally, you want to continue to breathe slowly, in and out, while making your intervention.

Now, instead of saying remember to breathe, I remind interveners "Remember to exhale." You will probably need to inhale first, but by focusing on an exhalation, your respiratory system will automatically inhale. Once I exhale, I find it very difficult to speak without taking time to inhale.

Mediator's Stance

The pause and exhale techniques offer a moment to gain control of your breathing and to notice how you are carrying your body. You might find your shoulders are pulled up to your ears, indicating tension. I have noted over the years that many women hold their arms folded and close to their chest. Men, on the other hand, will hold their arms down in front of their groin. Either position can be perceived as a protective stance.

Maintaining a neutral stance, such as the mediator stance, facilitates discussion and does not emit readiness for potential combat. The mediator's stance is a standing position that provides a non-threatening appearance as well as protection from possible attacks. The mediator's stance typically elects a left foot forward position because most people are right-handed. Our world is predominantly right-handed, so we can make the assumption that when people strike out, they are likely to lead with the dominant side, which is usually their right side (When intervening with a known left-handed person a right foot forward stance is advised.) If you sense potential physical danger, preventive measures like a left foot forward stance protects the most vulnerable part of your body—the vital organs and the face.

Mediator's Stance– Knees

Knees should be partially flexed. A slight bend in the knees makes it easier to move in toward a person or away. Imagine a ball player up at bat. Because the player is expected to run right after hitting the ball, there is a deep flex in the knees. The ball player's deep bend is not necessary for everyday conflict, though. A slight flex will do.

Mediator's Stance – Hand Position

Keep your hands level with your waistline. As for what to do with your hands, I prefer loosely grasping my hands without interlocking my fingers. I also find that holding my palms up as if holding a large book is an open and non-threatening gesture. Allow your hands to move slowly so you don't look stiff and uncomfortable.

Mediator's Stance – Forty-Five Degree Angle

Positioning yourself at forty-five degrees to the person with whom you are speaking provides a space for the agitated person to exit. When you physically block the way for a person to leave the room, as you would in a face-to-face confrontation, you compromise safety.

More on Self-control

Self-control is never more critical than during a crisis. Even if they don't seem to show it, people who are involved in the crisis as well as the onlookers are counting on you as intervener to act with self-assurance. This expectation applies to everyone, from parents to cashiers to fire fighters and other human service workers. Your stance, as well as your ability to speak with a clear and steady voice, directly impacts how those in conflict perceive your ability to manage a crisis.

Self-control at a Car Accident

As an EMT for sixteen years between 1981 and 1997, I was the first responder at the scenes of many car accidents. During times of intense crises, I have learned the value of maintaining self-control and the power of the pause and exhale.

I was on the way to visit my parents when traffic began to slow, and I realized that there was an accident up ahead. I was able to safely weave my way closer and park my car. Grabbing my case with medical supplies, I ran toward the scene and noticed that no official emergency vehicles were there yet. As I approached, I saw two damaged cars, one burning, with people scattering away from it. I also noticed uninjured people who I assumed had come from the nearby homes to help accident victims. I stood for a moment and took in the scene. Taking a couple of slow, deep breaths, I tried to plan my next move.

It would be about ten minutes before the first of four ambulances arrived. There were seven people injured. The most seriously injured were four Chinese exchange students who spoke little English. A drunk driver who had a baby and another passenger in her car had hit their vehicle.

I began going from injured person to injured person to assess their medical needs. When the ambulances finally arrived, I relayed the information to each of the four teams. The scene was chaotic, with the injured moaning from pain, so I reminded the caregivers to take slow, deep breaths so they would not get agitated themselves.

Once the injured were on their way to the hospital, I sat down off to the side. Slowly, all the nonprofessionals who were helping at the scene when I first arrived approached me. They thanked me for my help and guidance. I had thought that I was an invisible caretaker, unnoticed in the flurry of other emergency workers. I was surprised to hear how I had helped these good Samaritans focus on the task instead of getting caught up in the intensity of the disaster scene. They had noticed me when I first entered and stood silently to evaluate the scene. That presence of mind had set me apart. My calm had enabled others to find a quiet, inner place where they could function effectively. It served as a reminder that the crisis could and would be managed.

Any frantic energy I had felt slowed with my pause and exhale at the point of entry onto the accident scene. The impact of my pause was greater than I had expected and touched other caregivers who also needed reassurance.

In any intervention, personal safety is your first priority. With safety as your measuring stick, you know clearly when to enter or exit an intervention. You risk your own safety and that of others when you go blindly into a conflict without thinking first, "Am I safe?"

If you are not safe, the goal becomes—Make yourself safe.

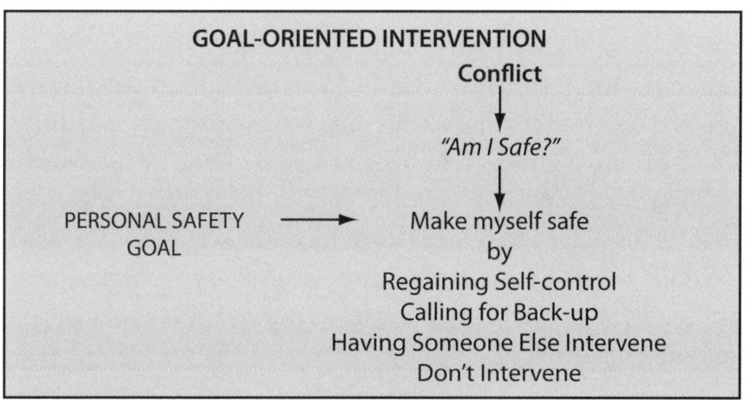

If, however, you are safe, then the next step is to ask yourself "Is the Scene Safe?" For now hold that train of thought until the next chapter, while we keep exploring personal safety and what to do when you are not safe.

How to Secure Personal Safety

Trying the pause and exhale one more time may be all that is needed to help regain a sense of well-being, self-control, and safety.

If the option is available, get someone else to be with you during the intervention. This person's role may vary from witnessing the event to actively engaging in management of the conflict to acting as a decoy for calling you away if the conflict escalates.

Using a Phone Call as an Exit Strategy

Professionals in the human service field use the technique of telling a staff member that they have a phone call as an exit. In the Response Crisis Intervention Model we encourage the use of a two-tiered exit strategy in using the phone call. To check in and see if the intervener needs assistance, a co-worker would say to the primary intervener, "You have a phone call." The primary intervener can exit if she needs to or tell her co-worker she will "call back" if she is feeling confident in her intervention.

The second-tiered exit with the phone is available for situations when the co-worker makes a decision to pull out the primary intervener who has become too emotionally caught up in the intervention. The second-tiered phone exit statement is, "The doctor is on the phone." This universal code means that the primary intervener has to leave the scene. Sometimes we don't realize how emotionally entangled we have become and need a helping hand to escort us out of a scene that is spiraling downward.

Non-professionals have mentioned that they might call their friend on the phone before a difficult conversation with a family member. They ask their friend to call them back in ten minutes once the family discussion begins. The callback serves as a break, allowing people to take a breather and maybe even discuss with the friend some options for managing the scene. In highly escalating conflicts, the police are called in for help.

When "Don't Intervene" is an Option

Bowing out of an intervention when someone is more qualified and able to intervene is a reasonable option when you feel unsafe. Determining your exit plan and adjusting yourself accordingly could provide a measure of safety so that you can continue with the intervention. Feeling literally backed up against a wall during a conflict can be a frightening experience. A small, cramped room or many, large obstacles blocking your exit to the door can make you feel unsafe even if you are a skilled intervener.

Not getting involved in the conflict in the first place may be the best option when feeling unsafe. However, if another person has targeted you directly, merely walking away may not be an option. In scenarios where you do not feel capable of managing the conflict, intentionally acquiescing to the antagonist may be the only alternative.

Under Attack and Unsafe

When a person is intent on attacking you verbally or physically, and you can neither escape the scene nor defend yourself, making a conscious choice to allow the person to continue with her rampage may be the only immediate option. Surrendering the scene or not engaging could mean simply standing still while a person berates you. If you are being physically attacked and are unable to defend yourself, curl up into a ball to protect your organs and face.

I mention the need to make a calculated surrender at times because of stories I have heard about people being critically injured during a physical attack. One form of calculated surrender may involve consciously making a choice to relinquish some level of control to an antagonist. This keeps a thread of scene control in your hands. Although it may seem insignificant and certainly wouldn't lessen the verbal or physical blows of such an attack, it will serve to maintain a sense of self-integrity rather than total surrender.

Summary: Take the Time to Ensure Personal Safety

Regardless of the amount of experience you have, it can be initially disorienting to hear the loud voice of an agitated person. Working long hours, being preoccupied with troubles at home, or simply being overwhelmed with the problem at hand can all contribute to poor decision-making and conflict escalation.

The natural "fight-or-flight" response will always be urging you to take a less-than-calculated conflict management approach. Self-leadership is crucial and necessary if you are truly seeking de-escalation.

It takes minimal time to assess whether you are safe. The pause and exhale are done simultaneously and take five seconds.

Despite the apparent simplicity of taking time to pause and exhale, the step will require practice. No need to despair, though. The technique provides an immediate sense of self-empowerment. The pause can allow you to manage conflict instead of being baffled by the task at hand. Your inner sense of well-being will likely become contagious. Those who are caught up in emotional turmoil seek those who are projecting a sense of calm and well-being. Say "Ahhhhh" and exhale, and you will be on the right path.

Is the Scene Safe?

Wisdom consists in being able to distinguish among dangers and make a choice of the least harmful.

— Niccolo Machiavelli

Common sense should advise you to be wary before proceeding into a chaotic scene. Yet many people throw caution to the wind. Anyone who feels immune to getting hit when stepping between two fighters, for instance, may realize in hindsight that sheer luck kept harm away.

A scene that is visibly chaotic, emotionally charged, and potentially volatile is not safe, regardless of other factors. Approach such conflicts with calculated caution. Instead of being swept away by the ensuing hysteria of emotions, learn to view a scene objectively.

Scene Safety Assessment:

The Feel, Look, Listen Approach Revisited

Once personal safety is attained, the next step is to appraise the level of safety in the surrounding environment: feel the mood or tension in the room, look for visual indicators, and listen for auditory cues. This stage begins with the question "Is the Scene Safe?".

"Is the Scene Safe?"

↓

Feel

Acknowledge your intuitive sense.

What feels safe? What doesn't feel safe?

Look

Observe the whole scene.

Does something or someone seem out of place?

Listen

Ascertain what is being said.

What is the overall timbre of voices in the room?

If there is a conflict, even a minor one then the scene is considered unsafe. The scene safety goal is to "Make the Scene Safe".

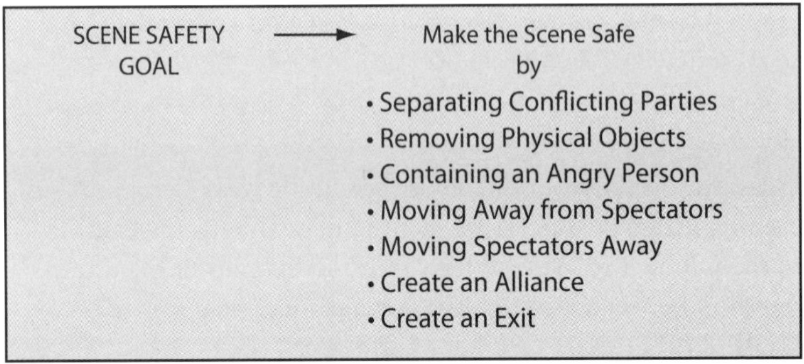

Make the Scene Safe: Separate Conflicting Parties

The quickest way to secure scene safety is by separating the conflicting parties. Using a verbal prompt to distract two angry people, for instance, is a common technique. "Michael, come on. Let's get out of here and take a break." This prompt may be all that is needed to pull someone out of a conflict.

Depending upon your authority or relationship to those involved in a conflict, the verbal prompt may differ. For instance, a parent, a teacher, or a police officer may use authority to demand instant separation with the expectation that they will be listened to: "Break it up, you two!"

If you are intervening with complete strangers, a more neutral and aligning statement is necessary. Personal safety is of the utmost importance in such a case due to the possibility of personal attack. A verbal prompt such as "Walk with me, please," if done in a sincere and strong tone, has been sufficient at times to separate someone from a conflict.

Make the Scene Safe: Remove Objects

Removing objects that may hinder movement can help to make a scene safe. Toys on the floor, chairs blocking an exit or movement, and similar large and small objects can be hazards. Moving items to the side or out of the room entirely can set a tone of spaciousness and safety. People are less likely to feel cramped and bothered by a room that allows movement and contains fewer stimuli.

Make the Scene Safe: Containing an Angry Person

Containing someone who is volatile is not necessarily done as a physical intervention. Asking or telling a person to take a "time-out" is a widely used technique. Parents may send their child to her room or a safe corner, away from spectators and antagonists. Human service workers use the question, "Do you want a time-out?" when directing an angry person to pause and stop certain behaviors. Many educators set aside a space in the classroom for students who need a little quiet time to reflect and regain a sense of self-control.

Make the Scene Safe: Managing Spectators

Spectators can incite further violence. There are two options available when spectators are involved: you can move away from the onlookers, or you can move the onlookers away. Removing onlookers decreases the tendency for angry parties to perform as if in front of an audience. Again, depending upon your relationship to the onlookers, the task may or may not be difficult. As a rule of thumb, spectators will be more willing to move away without question when directed by an authority figure.

People's images precede them when they have a particular role. A teacher, for instance, by virtue of her job, is an authority figure that can act in a positive manner to direct an environment that is conducive to learning. The students' expectations are that she will be capable, even before they meet her, because she is in the role of a teacher.

Your Authority

"Never underestimate the amount of authority that you have by virtue of your job and who you are as a person" is an old saying of mine that I find is worth repeating from time to time. It has been my experience that people forget that they are looked to as the "one in charge," whether they are at work, at home, or just an adult who happens to see a group of youngsters bullying another child. When I say this short phrase at a seminar, participants slowly shake their heads as if remembering a long forgotten memory. We are all responsible and capable of making our world safe. Authority is not necessarily measured by how loudly you speak or by how many people you command, but by the intent behind your actions.

There is a fine balance between using and abusing the power of authority. By and large, humans are extremely perceptive. We sense when we are being abused, manipulated, or coerced and are less likely to willingly comply. On the other hand, I have noticed that when a person assumes a position of authority and speaks with clarity and compassion, most people listen and readily follow that person's directives.

At the Roadside Speaking to the Angry Crowd

The night was pitch black and the roads were slick with ice as I made my way home after an evening class. About a mile from my house, I noticed a bit of traffic ahead and knew intuitively that there had been an accident. I pulled my car off to the side of the road. Stepping quickly out of the car, I slipped and fell flat on my back. With a thud I landed. "Ouch!" I cried out to no one in particular. Carefully and slowly, I rose. I would have to walk at least twenty-five yards to the scene ahead and seriously considered getting into my car and going home. My attention was caught, however, when I heard angry voices and saw someone lying in the middle of the road. "All right," I said to myself. "You're not hurt. Now go forward and see if you can help."

As I approached, I saw a number of men yelling at two other men, one who was sitting in his car and another who was lying on his back in the middle of the road. I recognized these men, but didn't know any of them personally. I could see that one young man was focused on the person lying on the road. He was saying something like, "I'm gonna teach you a lesson, you drunk. Look at what you two idiots did to my car!" I observed the crowd, none of whom was ready to intervene. I felt the timing was right for me to step in out of the dark.

"I'm an EMT. I'll check out this man," I called out. The all-male crowd stepped back as I moved into the slight glow from surrounding headlights. The angry young man said that the guy lying down wasn't worth it. "I have my job to do," I replied. With slow and cautious steps, I moved next to the man lying on the road. He yelled a babble of angry words. Looking down at the shivering man, I said, "I am not the enemy. I am here to help." The surrounding voices grew quiet, and I proceeded to check the man on the road.

In the end, no one was hurt, and only vehicles had been damaged by the slight fender bender. When the police cruiser arrived, I made my exit. Once again, I appreciated the value of taking my time, observing the scene first to ensure my own safety, and speaking with authority and compassion. I was able to move the focus of attention away from anger and toward de-escalation, by stating my position, not getting involved with the conflict (dropping the content), and being a voice of reason.

However, I didn't do such a great job assessing personal safety, when I first arrived. I can still feel the thud of my own body falling onto the icy ground. I had carelessly stepped out too soon. Here was a concrete reminder to slow down. I was overzealous and in helper mode. Helper mode is dangerous if you forsake personal safety. If I had assessed the scene before getting out of my car, I would have noticed the black ice and been more careful.

It has never ceased to surprise me that people listen when I speak up in a clear and concise fashion during a volatile scene. I have been granted authority by virtue of being the one who steps forward to offer a reasonable option to those in conflict. Violence and nonviolence both stand out, but they send two distinctly different messages. The first is a beacon for chaos, while nonviolence signifies inner calm and control. Such presence sets a tone of leadership and self-control.

My lasting memory of that night—and a lesson well learned—is that interventions should only be done if personal safety is secured.

Create an Alliance

Create an alliance that identifies you as working for the common good of those involved in the conflict. This role requires the ability to project neutrality. You might be scratching your head and wondering how you can create an alliance while maintaining neutrality. The answer is that you ally yourself with the goal of working for the common good of those involved in the conflict. An intervener maintains this position by avoiding face-to-face confrontations. Standing face-to-face with a person who is angry can make you a target. This is where the mediator's stance comes in.

What Is Your One-liner?

The first words spoken by an intervener set the stage for the rest of the intervention. When emotionally distraught or consumed by rage, we can only hear a few words at a time. Personally, I hope that the person will hear my "Hello," "Thank you," and "Good Job" statements rather than words and phrases such as "Stop," "Calm down," or "Shut up." Remember the phrase the angry person is "drunk on his own rage"? Instead of alcohol, the intoxicant is rage. Until the rage subsides, that person will not be able to hear more than one to four words. This might seem and sound logical and easy, but making what we refer to in the Response Crisis Intervention Model as a "One to Four Worded Intervention" does require practice.

Avoid Interpretive Statements

Everyone's life experience is different, and should be respected as such. Therefore, avoid using interpretive statements like, "I understand that you are angry." The term "I understand" is a common phrase used by professionals and nonprofessionals when speaking to an upset or angry person. You may want to try to understand how you can help someone who is having difficulty, but can you really understand another person's experience? Even if you had a similar episode in your own life, it is unique to your own experience. This is a subtle concept, yet it is very powerful. Many people don't notice the difference; but if there is a choice for a more refined option, why not try it? Instead of saying "I understand," you could try "I would like to understand." Words are powerful, and this small shift is an opening that signifies a willingness to hear more versus the first statement, which could be taken as, "I have heard it all before."

I find that creating an alliance helps me to achieve scene safety quickly because I am working with the group instead of trying to control the group. I first wrote about the following scenario for *Aikido Today Magazine*. It is an actual intervention that demonstrates the use of creating an alliance in order to make a scene safe.

Creating an Alliance at the Campground

It was a Friday afternoon, and I was elated. My friends and I were going camping together for three days. When we arrived at our site, a flurry of activity took place as we quickly set up camp. I was holding up a pole for a large tarp to go over the picnic table when I heard the chilling statement, "I am going to kill you." It was then that I saw the twenty-something man who had made the threat. He was stomping across the campground toward a site that was filled with other young people who were taunting him. One young woman in that group grabbed her crotch in a sexually explicit way as if to say, "You jerk, this is what I think of you."

Across from us where another family was camping, I saw the mother grab her small child as she ran into her tent. I noticed a look of horror in her eyes and recognized her desire to flee. My friends and I stood for a moment, and I decided to act. At least I felt personally safe from harm, since I was not the target of the man's threat and I had seen no weapons. The scene was becoming more and more volatile as threats flew between the group and the angry young man.

I began by walking slowly toward the young man and the group of antagonists who had surrounded him. "No fighting here. There are children," I called out in a steady and repetitive fashion. Another woman camper across from me also chimed in, "No fighting." She stopped far away from the group, but I kept on walking toward them with my chant, "No fighting here. There are children."

I felt like the eye of a hurricane as I moved in closer to the group and they parted to let me pass. It became obvious to me that my slow and steady movements and words were impacting the entire group. Perhaps some of the participants were taken by surprise that not everyone was enticed by the potential mob mentality of wanting a fight. Others became curious to see what I was up to and if others would listen. I felt an alliance with those who parted before me and allowed me to go through. No one told me to get lost. The antagonistic group became speechless as I drew closer. I moved up alongside the angry young man and his final target, a man his own age. I had no desire to stand between the two of them and risk being their next target. The two were yelling at each other and threatening to fight. I turned to the young man who had first threatened to kill the other and said, "Walk with me, please."

As if by magic, he turned away, and we stepped together out of the chaos and toward the road. The group again parted and let us out of the circle. The man stopped and turned back for a moment when the crowd teased him about walking away. "Water over the dam," I said, and we kept walking. "You are doing great. Let's keep moving," I encouraged. When we had reached a measurable distance of safety from the group, and I no longer felt he would turn back to their taunts, I said, "I would like to hear all about it." The young man's eyes flooded with tears, and he began to tell me a story of lost love and hardship as we made our way back to his camp.

I left him at his campsite with a small circle of his own friends and told them to keep him safe. The rest of the weekend was trouble-free. The group of antagonists left soon after my intervention. My new friend and I saw each other across the way from time to time and passed a wave or a nod of the head.

In the situation I just described, with my personal safety intact, I was able to commit myself to making the scene safe. My movements and positioning were calculated. I created an opportunity for those too confused by the growing conflict to align with me instead of the mob. I used concrete phrases that were non-threatening and truthful—there were children all over the place, and it wasn't the time to fight. I reminded everyone that they could be responsible if they chose to be.

I didn't ask the crowd to move away because their focus was on the angry young man and what he would do next. The area was pretty clear of obstacles, and I wasn't about to move any trees. Getting physical was not my first choice, and that is what I would have had to do to attempt to contain the young men. My only real choice was to try to align with the parties involved, as previously discussed (find a common goal for the good of all), and show them an alternative to violence. If I had waited until the park ranger appeared, the fight might have already started and ended with someone getting hurt. Asking the young man to walk away "Created an Exit"—a reason to step away.

If the group had not parted and let me through, I would not have gone into the circle. Since the group did open up quite a bit of space to allow me to pass, I took this as a sign that they accepted my role and were willing to work with me on my terms. They were also very likely dumbfounded and curious about this woman walking slowly towards them. They were the cobras and I was the snake charmer. Instead of a flute, I used a universal truth, "No fighting. There are children."

Instead of saying too much, as in, "Hey, you guys, no fighting here. Can't you see that there are children? This is a campground, not a boxing ring," I repeated a short and simple phrase, what I call a "One to Four Worded Intervention" over and over. Not only did my words catch the spectator's attention, but they showed how focused I was on the event. I wasn't acting as one more cog in the wheel. My concentration on the incident made it clear to others that I was in for the duration of the conflict.

Once scene safety is achieved, you can build upon the alliance you have created and work with the parties involved toward the goal of helping those in conflict regain a sense of self-control.

When Personal and Scene Safety Are No Longer At Risk

With personal safety and scene safety secured, options for resolving conflict can be discussed. Beware though of confusing conflict resolution as used in mediation versus resolution during a crisis. The "Conflict Resolution Goal" for a crisis intervener is—confirm scene safety. Too often interveners begin to discuss the conflict with an angry party before the scene is indeed confirmed safe. Consider the protocol used by firefighters and that of other response teams. A fire might look like it is out because the obvious flames are extinguished, but the fire is not officially declared out, until the Fire Marshal deems it is so. The same is true after a natural disaster like an earthquake. The building might look safe to enter, but until the building is confirmed safe by structural engineers, entering the building too quickly is very dangerous.

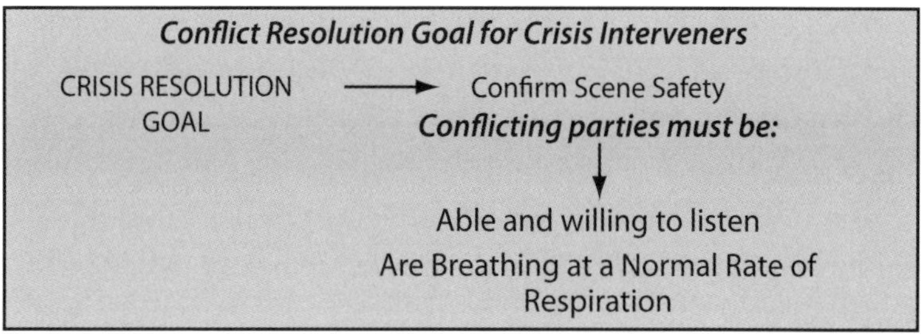

Everyone involved in the conflict must be in agreement for working a conflict out, meaning that they are willing to listen and not interrupt others. Until that point, resolution cannot be considered. Crisis resolution may happen simultaneously while the scene is being made safe, afterwards when tempers have been quieted, or not at all.

You may initially make an area safe only to find that tempers reheat, and the intervention cannot continue until you again address safety issues. All you can do is keep going back to your initial goal of creating a safe environment, and in the process, keep working toward de-escalation. Having a clear set of questions to ask yourself as you move through the intervention—Am I safe? and Is the scene safe?—helps to maintain our focus and provides a proactive model for making the scene safe for all. The following examples illustrate this point.

Ricky and John's Fight

Ricky and John Martin were pushing each other in the Martins' backyard. The pushing quickly turned into punching. Both parents ran to the scene from opposite directions, with Mr. Martin arriving first. While separating the two boys, Mr. Martin asked, "Okay, who started it?"

Both boys screamed out in unison, "He did!" and then, "You liar!"

Here, Mr. Martin's personal safety was not at risk. The scene, though, was not safe. Instead of making the scene safe, Mr. Martin's first inclination was to find out what happened. Who doesn't want to get to the root of the problem? People, by and large, are kindhearted and want to help. But, be very careful of providing the wrong type of help during an intervention.

It is best to drop the content and let people sort through their mess once the scene is safe, but here, instead, Mr. Martin's question only agitated the boys further. His intervention was bad for Mr. Martin and bad for his boys.

Instead of getting the two boys to settle down, they both became more agitated when their father asked who had started it. This simple question actually incited the scene further as they both vied for their father's attention and defended their views. It is a resolution question that shouldn't be used until the scene is safe for everyone. Questioning the two boys should have taken place only after Ricky and John had been separated and given time to settle down.

Interventions like this one take place every day, with a person trying to resolve the conflict first. But such interventions involve a level of coercion providing only a short-term solution. Instead, emphasize safety and provide an alternative to the "might-makes-right" style of confrontational conflict management.

Addressing Ricky and John's Personal Safety

People are less inclined to be truthful or willing to compromise when they feel threatened. Giving each boy some time alone, away from his brother, might facilitate Ricky and John's individual needs to be personally safe from harm. Securing personal safety and scene safety is an important prerequisite for sound crisis resolution.

Instead of asking the two boys, "Who started the fight?" Mr. Martin could instead begin by saying, "Okay, let's all settle down." He could then either direct the boys to take a "time-out" or, if they were visibly de-escalating, he might be able to walk them away from the immediate scene. Finding a neutral location like a picnic table or other sitting area could help to set the mood for discussing the fight and also allow the warring parties to work things out under parental supervision. Mr. Martin could ask the boys to speak one at a time and set a goal for them. "We are a family," he could say, "and sometimes we don't get along. Still, it is hard to see my two sons fighting. Let's try talking about what happened without being mean to each other." He could ask each boy if he agrees to work with his brother: "Ricky, are you willing to discuss this matter now?" and then, "John, how about you? Can you discuss this matter now, also?" Such an approach would set an expected norm of civility for the ensuing discussion.

Mr. Martin could also state what the goal of the discussion was: to work through a conflict without being mean. Helping his sons learn problem solving early on is a life skill that will take them through adulthood.

Like the previous situation, not all interventions are high risk for the intervening party. Yet, many people work at sites where personal safety can be threatened. The following vignette illustrates what can happen when the intervener is focused more on stopping the conflict than on ensuring personal and scene safety.

Joan's Overreaction

The halfway house for incarcerated women had been quiet for most of the evening. From her office, Joan could hear the steady murmur of the television down the hall. Louise, the only other staff person on duty, was in the basement helping a resident with her laundry. Joan first heard Helen's voice yell out, "Don't change that channel, girl!"

Chris replied, "You're not watching anything. You've got your nose in the magazine!"

Joan jumped out of her chair and ran down the hall. While running down the hall, she yelled out, "Hey, knock it off in there!" Joan took no time to stop at the door and look in. She kept moving until she was next to Chris, who was standing over Helen, her finger pointed in Helen's face. With the background noise of the television, Joan's voice grew louder as she said, "What is going on here? Who was watching first?"

Tamara, Gwen, and Pearl, also in the room, took the opportunity to chime in their own thoughts about who should watch what.

What was Joan's Goal: Crisis Intervention or Crisis Resolution?

Joan's intervention is typical of someone who thinks she is making an intervention but by virtue of the words she chooses—"Hey, knock it off in there!" —moves right into stop mode/resolution. She actually incited further agitation. As a result of the ensuing chaos, Joan would now, unfortunately, have to work even harder since there were, by the end, five people involved instead of the original two She allowed herself to get off-track from what should have been her primary task, which was to ensure personal and scene safety. The program on the television was of little importance, yet Joan went along with the residents in making it the focal point. Joan's intervention only served to reinforce the explosive model of reacting to conflict with emotionally-guided behavior.

Was Joan Thinking About Safety?

Joan had moved directly into the room without assessing the scene. If Joan had paused at the doorway to take in her surroundings, she might have been able to de-escalate this conflict quickly without risking her own safety, but her main goal had been to take control in an authoritative manner by demanding that the group "knock it off in there!" before she even had any idea what was actually going on between Helen and Chris. Stepping into the middle of the conflict between Helen and Chris was a reactive response on Joan's part and could easily have set her up as the target of the group's anger.

Joan and other interveners who react to a conflict instead of act in response to the conflict do so because they feel that something must be done quickly. In this case, she would have been better off being proactive instead of reactive in order to ensure the quick solution she was aiming for. Being proactive would have allowed her to stay calm and clearheaded. Not only would Joan have felt in control of herself, but she would have been better able to view the choices available to her for managing the scene, instead of demanding and shouting statements in a threatening manner.

How Could Joan's Intervention Be Improved?

If Joan had paused and at the very least addressed the other residents by either nodding to signify her control of the scene or by saying, "Could you three please step out of the room?" she would have set up an alliance with them and distanced them from the primary conflict. They could ignore her or refuse her request, but by acknowledging them before moving on to Helen and Chris she could have both noted their presence and given them a choice.

On their end, Tamara, Gwen, and Pearl were doing their part to escalate the conflict. Acknowledging the entire scene, not just Helen and Chris, would have shown the rest of the residents that Joan was able to manage multiple tasks and wasn't completely consumed by the crisis at hand.

People want to feel safe. Interveners who project confidence and self-control present a convincing authority and a can-do attitude. People in the middle of a crisis are more likely to submit to a person who appears levelheaded than to an intervener who is frantic.

Sally's Intervention

> *The sky was turquoise on an early December afternoon as Sally walked through the front door of her home on Cleary Street. Before she even took off her overcoat, she heard her oldest daughter Clara, a senior in high school, screaming at her younger sister, "Doris, give me back my shirt!"*
>
> *Doris came running out into the hallway toward her mother. She had a purple shirt in her hands. Flying out the door behind Doris came a plastic cup that hit the wall across the carpeted hall. "I'm going to kill you!" cried Clara. With eyes wide, Doris said to her mother, "She's going crazy again, Mom. This isn't her shirt, and I'm not gonna give it to her!"*
>
> *Clara walked into the hall with her slipper raised above her head and her other hand clenched into a fist. Upon seeing her mother with Doris, she wailed, "Get away from Mom."*

This scenario all happened in less than half a minute. Sally had stepped right into a cross fire of physical threats and verbal assaults. She hadn't done so on purpose. She had been merely returning home from work. The goals of personal safety and scene safety would nevertheless need to prevail.

Sally's first goal should have been safety for herself and her two daughters. It didn't matter whose shirt was whose. Trying to solve that mystery would have to wait until after Doris and Clara had gained control of themselves and could listen, and Clara seemed especially "over the edge" or "drunk on her own rage." Sally would only escalate the crisis if she tried to converse with the two girls about shirts and ownership. The main concern is always to make sure that no one is hurt and that threats are not allowed to come to fruition.

Watching the scene unfold, Sally is in a good position to figure out a few possible goals. She needs to pause and exhale in order to think more clearly. She knows there is a risk to safety because Clara has threatened Doris and is holding one hand raised with a potential weapon and the other balled up into a fist. Sally's first goal is to separate the two girls so that they cannot continue their mutual antagonism. After talking separately with Doris and Clara, Sally might be able to facilitate a discussion between the two teenagers about the conflict or ownership of the shirt. Let's see what effect Sally might have on this crisis.

Sally's Intervention Continues

> *"Doris, I want you to go down the hall and wait for me in my bedroom, please," says Sally.*
>
> *"Mom!" cries Clara while taking a step closer to her mother. "You can't..."*
>
> *Sally cuts her oldest daughter off in mid-sentence and says, "Clara, that slipper belongs on the floor and not in the air." Clara slowly brings down her hand with the slipper. Sally continues speaking softly to her daughter. "You are awfully upset. I want to hear what has been going on. Let's go into the kitchen. I'll set us up some milk and cookies."*
>
> *"I don't want any stinking cookies!"*
>
> *"Okay, but I sure need something, and I would like to sit down and hear your side of the story first."*

Doris was sent to her mother's room. Before trying to move Clara out of the hallway, Sally was able to set a clear boundary with her oldest daughter by asking her to put the slipper down.

Her soft-spoken style and nurturing manner created an alliance with Clara, or at least reassured Clara that she had not taken sides. If Sally had tried setting a boundary by saying, "Don't you raise your hand to your sister, young lady! Put that arm down! Right now!" no neutrality could be assured. Clara might have continued to move past her mother in order to get to her sister. As it worked out, Sally could now excuse herself for a moment from Clara to check in on Doris.

In summary, Sally's take-charge attitude enabled her to set boundaries and helped define her authority as the mother. Her attitude asserted that she would be the one to decide how conflicts were handled and the one who clarified the boundaries and rules.

Importance of Scene Safety

Making the scene safe often means having to separate two parties in conflict. The separation immediately accomplishes two goals: safety and de-escalation. If there is no one to argue with, an aggressor's anger may be redirected. A time-out or time away will enable parties to rethink ways to work through conflict without getting violent. By taking away the target of someone's anger, you instantly create a safer environment.

De-escalation and safety are often prompted by the mere presence of an authority figure. Each of us has experienced the schoolteacher who can walk into a chaotic classroom and calm everyone solely by her presence or stern look. Parents and direct care staff can use the same nonverbal technique, conveying without a doubt that the dispute must stop. The effectiveness of someone's presence is based on authority and the ability to create an alliance, as well as the ability of those in conflict to de-escalate nonviolently.

Knowing Your Personal Boundaries

Having a clear sense of personal boundaries helps make a scene safe. Personal boundaries vary depending upon cultural background, ethnicity, family upbringing, and past experiences. How close you allow someone to move toward you or what you feel is appropriate language are personal preferences and set your personal boundaries. A lack of clear boundaries can make everyone involved feel unsafe. A scene does not have to be volatile to feel unsafe and threaten boundaries. The next vignette illustrates how easily a boundary can be crossed.

Uncle Jake's Disregard for Personal Boundaries

Uncle Jake's drunken antics at family gatherings were well-known by all. He liked to make loud, obnoxious announcements like "Hey, who wants to tease Aunt Jean?" It wasn't unusual for him to start loudly singing lyrics to old sailing songs, such as "Shave his belly with a rusty razor… …Put him in the hold with the Captain's daughter," that would make everyone feel uncomfortable, especially in front of the children.

Newcomers to a gathering were typically pulled to the side and forewarned about his behavior. Julienne somehow missed her pre-warning and was taken by surprise when Uncle Jake walked up to her and said, "How about a big hug for me?" and then promptly gave Julienne a big kiss on the lips.

Julienne said later to her boyfriend, who was Uncle Jake's nephew, "I saw him going around the room and doing the same thing to everyone. I knew he was eventually going to make his way to me, and I was going to be prepared. But then he was there, and I just didn't know what to do. I wanted to turn my face away, but I felt frozen. I wish I had just put up my hand and told him to stop. I have never met anyone like him before!"

Julienne could have done exactly what she wished. Everyone is allowed to set his or her own boundaries. Boundary setting lets the person you are interacting with know what you find permissible for her to do or say to you. You can convey your boundary verbally or nonverbally. To demonstrate, find a partner who will walk toward you from across the room. At some point, the other person will begin to enter your personal space. You may be inclined to say, "Stop!" as she gets closer. Nonverbally, your head might retract like a turtle's head going into its shell. People with strong communication skills need only the nonverbal gesture to know that they are too close. For people with no concept of personal boundaries, clear verbal information is needed for them to realize they have crossed a boundary.

What feels like an acceptable interaction to one person may feel like an intrusion to someone else. Being able to define your own boundaries is as important as paying attention to another person's boundary. Boundary setting can be difficult if you are not used to asking for what you want. An example is, "I hate it when Marsha expects me to hug her each time she sees me. But I feel awkward telling her, like I have a problem with intimacy." No need to feel awkward. We all have a right to protect our personal space and boundaries—go ahead tell Marsha, "No offense, but I'm not comfortable with hugs. How about a handshake?"

Yolanda's Lesson in Boundary Setting

Every fall, new people were hired to offset the high turnover of employees at Forest Residential Treatment Center. Unfortunately, the staff development position had been cut from the budget, so orientation to policies and the program was all done on-the-job. Yolanda knew she would be working with adjudicated adolescents, placed at F.R.T.C. by the courts for misdeeds like burglary or assault. She also knew she would have to be firm with them. After raising five boys of her own, she felt confident in her skills at working with extreme behaviors. What Yolanda didn't know was how to set boundaries as a direct care staff person working in a therapeutic milieu.

Yolanda's lack of training became evident to her when she asked Henry to wait his turn to use the pay phone. Henry quickly got within inches of Yolanda's face and pointed his finger down at her nose. "I got a right as much as anybody else here to use this phone. You're just new here and don't know the rules yet."

"Well, you may be right, Henry," Yolanda said. "I am new here, but I do know that Chris has two more minutes to use the phone and then it will be your turn." Henry began to respond until he heard the voice of Michele Gordon, the director of the house, yell from behind Yolanda, "Henry! Back away now!"

Later, during a meeting, Yolanda learned the residents were not allowed to approach staff so closely, since most of the residents had a history of violence, possibly including assault. Michele explained to Yolanda that, before any dialogue with an agitated person, she should first ensure her own safety. When Henry was initially approaching Yolanda, she could have raised her hands and asked him to stand back. Since Yolanda didn't stop Henry, who had no concept of respect for boundaries, he kept getting closer to her and disregarded her even more by pointing his finger in her face.

Setting limits is as important for the staff member who may be feeling unsafe as it is for the client to see limit-setting modeled. Yolanda was shaken and embarrassed to realize that she had put herself in a potentially dangerous situation.

This scenario and the one with Uncle Jake both illustrate how easy it is for boundary violations to occur. I have often met people like Yolanda who have had close calls when intervening. They become embarrassed by their lack of knowledge and angry with themselves when they realize that their intervention escalated the conflict and put them at risk.

"I thought that if I told the person to move back, I would be infringing upon her rights and that I might get into trouble," said Carla, a new member of the direct care staff at a large psychiatric center for adults. "I was scared when she kept coming toward me, but I thought that if I told her to stop or moved away, she would think that I didn't care. Maybe she wouldn't have stopped, and then I don't know what I would have done."

Yolanda and Carla were putting their client's needs ahead of their own, although their clients would have actually benefited from explicit boundaries.

When Boundaries are Not Respected

Another problem arises when the person in crisis doesn't heed your request. This is a valid concern, and it became apparent to me while working on the first edition of this book. I received a phone call from a mental health agency for adults seeking training in conflict management. When I asked what the specific concerns were, I was told that a resident had recently attacked a worker. The worker had been beaten and stabbed by a male resident of the apartment building owned by the agency, which arranges housing for its clients. There is no central data system telling us how many such attacks occur, but in my mind, even one attack is too many.

Perhaps the attack could have been avoided if the woman had received adequate training. At the minimum, she could have learned how to protect her vital organs and her face by curling up into a ball and, if need be, using self-defense to fight back. Being a caretaker does not mean that you lose the right to reasonably defend yourself when being attacked. Even if her agency does not allow the use of physical holds for containing a volatile person, she still has the legal right of self-protection. Because she is a human service worker, there is always the risk of litigation if she chooses to defend herself. However, by not protecting herself in the instance described above, she nearly lost her life.

Even minimal training can provide you with an effective level of self-control, which will help you to think clearly and verbalize your boundaries. Modeling a proactive way to speak up for yourself when being overwhelmed by another person is helpful if you are still learning how to set boundaries. Many people have been abused physically, emotionally, or sexually, or are just plain shy and not necessarily skilled at setting limits for themselves. Others simply have no experience in boundary setting.

You Don't Have to be Superhuman!

Having an invincible mind set can also make you unsafe. We will refer to this as the "Superman Complex," implying an overly confident attitude that disregards personal safety. It occurs when you assume an attitude of perfection, of being able to extinguish a conflict with a single word, by leaping into a crisis without hesitation, and of always being "right" in the eyes of others. Don't forget, though. Even Superman has to be safety conscious: Kryptonite could kill him.

Those inclined toward the Superman Complex should remember that to be human is to be imperfect. It can be difficult to accept our imperfections when we hold ourselves up to such high expectations that there is no room for error.

Working through a crisis using problem-solving techniques teaches valuable lessons. For parents, teachers, and human service workers, nothing could be more counterproductive than rushing through a conflict. Such behavior only teaches others to develop the same bad habits themselves. Speaking to another person without resorting to an authoritative style, invincible demeanor, or threats is an important model for all to see. It shows that there is no need to resort to greater violence in order to manage a scene. Taking the time needed to work out a crisis is okay and even preferable. It is through the problem-solving process that we learn about others and ourselves.

Set Attainable Goals

What may seem like an attainable goal to one person may seem to another like building a skyscraper. As a child, I played a game called Giant Steps. One person would stand facing away from the group and say "Take one giant step then take three baby steps." The object was to be the first person to tag the speaker so it could be your turn to be in front. Not everyone would get to the speaker at the same time, because everyone's steps were a different size.

This childhood game suggests the difference between what different people see as attainable goals. Problems arise when we put our own expectations on someone else. In the child's game, everyone wanted to take the biggest giant steps. Bigger was better, since it got you that much closer to your goal. Giant steps were the way to go. Baby steps—well, you could take them or leave them. The moral of the story, however, is that small steps are important, too, in attaining your goals—being first matters only in the game. Persistence and all the little steps can sometimes outweigh any benefit that you may gain by using speed or shortcuts. We must recognize and reward small steps taken by those in conflict.

How does this apply to conflict management? Well, for instance, the next time you are intervening in a conflict, call out the names of those involved—Bonnie! or Jane! If Bonnie actually turns her head and looks at you, she has just taken a baby step.

Although Bonnie is focused on Jane, her ability to look to the intervener calling her name indicates her recognition of an opportunity to exit the conflict. This small step can and should be acknowledged later by saying something like, "Bonnie, that was great when you gave me eye contact despite your conflict with Jane. Thank you for listening." You can even suggest a bigger step for the future: "Next time when you look at me, try taking a step back."

Avoid the tendency to view only the negative aspects of a conflict. In the Chinese language, the symbol Ji (or Gee) represents both crisis and opportunity. Redefining a crisis as an opportunity to work on skills of communication and problem solving takes away the fearful perception of crises as situations to be avoided.

Setting attainable goals helps us to become more effective as interveners. To make the scene safe is an attainable goal, whereas resolving the conflict is not as easily achieved, since conflicting parties do not always want to compromise. When we recognize their importance, baby steps start feeling good and become self-perpetuating.

Superman may be able to leap tall buildings with a single bound, and that is why he is an action hero. We mere mortals can avoid the Superman Complex by appreciating the value of taking little steps. With small steps, we begin to reframe our expectations and feel more at ease. If you are authoritative, you may sometimes be able to take a giant step and quickly resolve a conflict by assuming total control, but a domineering style quickly wears down both you and those in conflict. Instead of just "fixing the problem," effective conflict management means learning how to actively work through a conflict.

Summary: Ensure Personal and Scene Safety

The initial goal of conflict-crisis intervention is to ensure personal and scene safety, even though accomplishing this goal will most likely be taking place during the most dangerous time of the conflict—the conflict escalation. It matters not whether the dispute is a quarrel between lovers, a fight on the schoolyard, or an explosive brawl among patrons at a local club; the same protocol of "safety first" (personal and scene safety) holds true.

Aikido's Contribution to Scene Safety

When I was first introduced to Aikido, I was told that if two Aikidoists met each other in battle, each would stand waiting for the other to attack. But there are no attacks in Aikido, so the two would wait indefinitely. The concept intrigued me and at the same time felt like a riddle. "Hmmm," I thought, "would they really stand there forever waiting for the other to attack?"

There is a practice in Aikido of learning to know when the attack will occur. Observing an adversary and learning to sense an imminent attack involves a certain degree of attention to the scene and is a part of scene safety assessment. In a similar manner, becoming aware of the scene and being ready with a clear head are important at initial stages of conflict management.

Aikidoists work to perfect a nonviolent approach, including avoidance of inciting violence. The very open stance I described earlier and what is called the mediator stance is a powerful tool to this end. During workouts when I have been called upon to attack another student of Aikido, I have had trouble executing a full attack because the person on the receiving end stands in such an open, non-threatening manner. I find I can't muster up the will to make a strong attack.

Finally, Aikidoists work continuously to seek non-reproachful alternatives for meeting violence. Through the practice of Aikido, which takes much skill and a willingness to work toward nonviolent solutions, I have learned many valuable lessons about scene safety.

Do the two Aikidoists stand there forever waiting for the other to attack? Mythologically—yes, they do.

Creating Order

The ultimate weakness of violence is that it is a descending spiral, begetting the very thing it seeks to destroy. Instead of diminishing evil, it multiplies it... Returning violence for violence multiplies violence.

— Martin Luther King, Jr.

With personal and scene safety secured, the next goal is to help a person (people) in crisis regain a sense of self-control. This chapter provides a bounty of techniques on how to assist people in crisis and to do so without meeting violence with greater violence.

Upholding an attitude of self-assurance and authority is a critical element in the application of any conflict-crisis intervention technique. A successful intervention has as much to do with your command (self control) of inner fear as with techniques.

Body language reveals fear in the form of tight shoulders, wide eyes, shaking voice, a flushed or sweating face, and speech like, "Uh, hmmm, well ..." When your body unexpectedly expresses one of the above fear responses, establish order: not external order, like scene safety, but internal order, self control. In other words—get back into your body.

Men and women alike are pressured to fit into a physical mold that doesn't quite work for those of us who aren't super model material. This constant pressure that many of us face daily to look just so impacts how we feel about our bodies. If you add a bit of stress serum to the equation, like walking into the middle of an explosive conflict, you get people who would like to intervene, but their faces or shoulders are squinched up or held tightly, signifying a deeper desire to "get the heck out of the kitchen when the pans are flying."

When surrounded by volatile chaos or facing a threatening person, I think, "Stay in my body." Evidently, I am not alone in feeling uncomfortable. I have worked with many adults who trip over their own feet. A couple of people have even fallen down as they lost their balance while trying to figure out how to step away from an agitated person during a role play, not even a real conflict. I have also seen interveners push other people away when they were frightened and then not remember having done so.

Establish internal order by practicing the pause and exhale. Once you have maintained a normal rate of respiration, address your physical positioning, or stance. Gaining familiarity with the way you hold your body when intervening decreases the likelihood that you will assume a defensive posture that elicits confrontation.

When I was new to conflict management, I never gave a second thought to how I was standing. I now realize that this often left me vulnerable. Feet squared off, I would take a face-to-face stance. In the direct line of sight, I became the new target for anger. In all, I presented myself as ill-equipped to handle a volatile scene.

The Dangers of an Open Stance in the Emergency Room

> *While working as a crisis clinician in the ER, I once intervened with a patient who was delusional and fearful. Seeking safety, she tried to lock herself in the bathroom. The head nurse on duty decided to take matters into her own hands and stepped in front of me to speak with the patient. This nurse had more than twenty-seven years of experience in the ER. Yet her overzealous and poorly thought-out attempt nearly resulted in serious injury.*
>
> *The nurse stood in an open stance in front of the door while the patient tried to pull the door closed. I happened to catch the door with my foot, which stopped the patient from pulling it shut. If the door had been closed, it would have*

inadvertently caused the coat hook attached to the door to hit the back of the nurse's head.

During my debriefing with the nurse afterwards, she was astonished to learn how close she had come to being impaled. She had unknowingly put herself at risk because of her unguarded stance. If she had worked with me, her team member, her risk of harm could have been reduced. Instead of stepping between the patient and me, a safer position would have been next to me, situating her out of the direct line of attack and the coat hook.

When you are emotionally involved in a crisis or feeling threatened, it is easy to lose yourself in the conflict. The nurse was oblivious to her face-to-face position. She was vulnerable to physical and verbal harm. An angry person will often vent anger at whoever is in front of her, so keep your body safe: you are the only one who can really do so without having to be rescued by others.

Stay within Sight But Out of Harm's Way

A highly agitated person can lose peripheral vision. The result is tunnel vision. He only sees what is directly in front of him or just off line from the center point of vision. It can be perplexing and downright aggravating when a person doesn't respond to you, even though you are standing side by side. It is important to realize that you are not necessarily being ignored—you are simply out his line of site. If you can't be seen, your intervention isn't going to work no matter how loudly you speak or what you say. Positioning yourself off to the side, but not alongside the person, in at least a forty-five degree angle to the person to whom you are speaking will help. Make sure you are in a protective stance, such as the mediator's stance described earlier. This positioning will help to ensure that you will be seen and heard without becoming a target.

This step is also part of creating an alliance, facilitating discussion instead of confrontation.

With practice, assuming the mediator's stance becomes an automatic response. You will look poised and focused with your body comfortable, relaxed, and protected. Those who are involved in the conflict will be drawn in by your projection of confidence.

"Those involved" in the conflict are the onlookers, antagonists, and scapegoats or targets. You sacrifice your own safety and the opportunity for positive role modeling when you address only the antagonist. Reassuring onlookers with a glance or nod validates scene safety and reinforces the "can-do" image of the intervener. Augmenting your actions with a verbal acknowledgment like "Hi, John," if you already know an onlooker, or just a soft "Hi" to a stranger instills a sense of teamwork and allegiance.

After intervening, I review my positioning, language, and level of focus. Did I set up an alliance? If so, I was right on target. At any time during my intervention, did I become the target of the other person's anger? If so, I need to step off the line and practice positioning.

I have now become so familiar with the mediator's stance that I naturally stand this way whether or not I am at risk. It is comforting to know that I can stand in a safe position while my mind is trying to manage the fight-or-flight response. If I do need to move quickly, my flexed knees are more likely to move than to lock up and freeze. And in the worst case scenario, my vulnerable body parts are protected from strikes or kicks.

You do not have to be working with a volatile population to appreciate a protective stance and the need to maintain a safe distance when faced with danger. Canoeing among alligators taught me the valuable lesson of respecting other's personal space and providing for an exit.

Everglades

One winter vacation, I went on a seven-day canoeing trip to the Ten Thousand Island section of the Florida Everglades. My friends and I decided to take some of the less traveled routes, which often led us to the resting spots of large, sun-soaked, sleeping alligators. When the current pushed the canoe toward the bank and a gator, we would have to paddle with skill to give a wide berth to the dozing reptile.

Big yellow, cat like eyes glared at us, whenever we came up close and personal to the giant reptile. Was it sleeping? Do alligators have eyelids? My pre trip research was lacking on alligators. What I did know was that getting close was not a good option. In what felt like an instant, a gator would fling him or herself into the water as our canoe rounded the bend and neared the skittish beast.

Alligators are timid and do not like to be boxed in with no exits. If you block their escape, you may find yourself capsized in the water with a gator!

Like an alligator, an angry person can flail and should be given a wide berth with plenty of room to move around. There was no need for us to challenge the gator, since it was doing no harm, just as there is no need to block a person if she is not endangering herself or others. The need to leave a scene is the flight side of the fight-or-flight response. Perhaps you can recall leaving a room at one time during an argument. Seeking to flee an uncomfortable scene is not unusual behavior. If a person leaves a scene only to take a break from the conflict, then there is really no reason to stop him from doing so. A time-out serves to give everyone a little breathing room. A break from conflict can be used to reflect on why there is a conflict or what you want to achieve by continuing the debate.

Seeking to flee in order to take a break or cool down is very different than seeking to flee a scene to cause harm. A person who leaves a conflict in order to seek revenge on someone else may need to be physically blocked from doing so. For example, a parent who is mediating a dispute between his two kids might stand in front of one child who threatens to leave the room to find the other and do something unwarranted. You might also need to consider physically stopping a person who, by leaving a conflict, risks harm to themselves or others. Physically stopping someone does not mean you have to necessarily stand in front of that person. Taking an intoxicated person's car keys is a proactive form of blocking an exit that potentially saves the intoxicated person and others from harm.

Creating Exits: Giving Control Back to the Person in Crisis

As a conflict management technique, creating an exit can be both physical and verbal. You can offer a physical exit by standing in a mediator's stance. This stance allows for quick exit for either party since you are not standing face to face, but rather off to the side of each other. Verbal exits may take the form of providing options or asking the person to consider options during a conflict. Open and inclusive statements acknowledge the ability of a person in crisis to think for herself and create an opportunity for a win/win outcome. These two elements unite the person in conflict and the intervener in the quest for reaching a common goal: maintaining or regaining self-control. An earlier example of this was the intervention at the campsite where I said, "Walk with me, please." This statement provided an exit and gave the angry young man a very tangible thing to do— to walk.

The Selective Use of Confrontation as a Management Technique

Confrontation does not provide an exit, nor does it elicit a conciliatory response from a person in conflict. This does not mean, however, that confrontation is ineffective and should never be used. On the contrary, under the right circumstances confrontation can be the quickest and most appropriate intervention. For instance, "John! Sit down now!" is a directive that when said with an authoritative intonation may get John to sit right down. The limitation of this style is that it quickly loses its impact when overused. It is a domineering approach toward problem solving. Confrontation is focused on stopping the behavior rather than helping those involved in the conflict feel safe or gain skills. The win/lose outcome typical of confrontation creates an adversarial dynamic between parties.

Understanding the Roots of Anger and Aggression

Dr. Barry J. Nigrosh's 1983 article, "Physical Contact Skills in Specialized Training for Prevention and Management of Violence," refers to the fear of loss of self-control as a generalized cause of anger or aggression. Dr. Nigrosh wrote, in essence, that an attack or violent episode gives a brief moment of power and, hence, relief from hopelessness, but the same episode also causes internal anxiety. If you believe, then, that an angry or aggressive person is reacting out of the fear of loss of self-control, then the solution is to find avenues to help the angry person regain some semblance of control.

Herein lies the biggest challenge for interveners: giving control to those in conflict without giving up control of the situation. For an enraged person, gaining self-control at the height of emotional turmoil is no small task. Giving people options puts the ball back in their court and helps them feel empowered.

Redirecting Sean's Fear of Loss of Self-control

Sean had just arrived at the halfway house for men in transition from jail to the open community. He had to stay there for the next three months and follow all the rules of the home. One of the toughest rules was a 9:00 PM curfew.

After one week, Sean was already testing the limits of the curfew. He had gotten off the phone with a friend who told him that his girlfriend was seeing another guy. After hanging up, Sean was ready to head out the door, but it was 9:00 PM.

If he left, he would be in violation of the rules and would have to return to jail and finish his sentence there.

The staff were not expected nor authorized to use physical force to stop residents. Marty, the staff person on duty that night, was sitting in the lounge with other residents. Sean called out, "Marty, I gotta go talk with my girl. I'll be back later."

Marty got up from the couch and walked over to the front door of the house while Sean was putting on his jacket. "It's after nine, Sean. Can't you speak with her tomorrow?"

"She's at some guy's house, and if I don't get there tonight, who knows what will happen?" Sean replied.

"Are you going to throw away all your hard work? What else can you do right now?" Marty asked.

"So I go back to jail," Sean replied.

"Think about it for a minute, Sean. Right now you can taste freedom; it's so close. I don't think you really want to throw it all away," Marty said. "Come on into the office, Sean. Let's keep talking."

"Man! I can't just let this girl go!"

"This is about you right now, Sean. Being on probation is hard work."

Sean looked at Marty, who continued speaking to Sean about how hard he had worked to earn an early release from jail.

Marty was simultaneously taking care of Sean's self-image and acknowledging his ability to make the right decision. He could have stated, "You know the rules. You leave now, and you're going right back to jail." This statement, while entirely true and to the point, would have provided no initiative or recourse for Sean. If Sean were able to make it through his first obstacle at the halfway house, he would have begun the process of learning how to maintain self-control.

Conflict management provides an opportunity to demonstrate proactive problem solving and behavior management techniques. Confrontation, on the other hand, takes the responsibility for self-control away from the person in crisis and puts it all on the intervener. It is a short-term solution to a long-term problem. Initiating opportunities for the person in conflict to attempt to regain self-control is time-consuming and effort-intensive, but the long-term gains are worth the effort. By offering an opportunity to regain self-control, interveners create a relationship—even if momentary—that allows them to become allies instead of adversaries. Thus, the intervener can remain in dialogue with conflicting parties and be a model for non-aggressive techniques.

Explosive Behavior and the Fear of Loss of Self-Control

In the clinical setting, correctional site, or school system, there is explosive behavior every day due to the fear of loss of self-control.

The following examples illustrate this kind of explosive behavior.

Example 1 – Explosive Behavior

A client was talking on the phone to a relative. The relationship between the two was strained, and the client ended the conversation by slamming the receiver down while shouting expletives into the mouthpiece. Later, the client explained that he had been told he wasn't welcome home for the holidays and that had been the cause for his outburst. Unable to control his family's wishes, he lashed out verbally at the relative and physically at the inanimate object, the telephone.

Example 2 – Explosive Behavior

In a correctional facility, an inmate was told that her weekend furlough had been rejected. The inmate responded by standing up, knocking over a chair, and threatening to assault the social worker.

Example 3 – Explosive Behavior

In school, a student threatened to do bodily harm to a teacher when he received an unfavorable report card. The student may actualize his threat by going home and getting a weapon.

Each scenario describes an outburst that can be attributed to feelings of hopelessness and fear of loss of self-control. If a person does not have the skills for channeling his despair or rage, a violent outburst is likely. Alternately, if the person has some skills, he may start to cry or go to his room, reorient himself, and emerge later to discuss the call with the staff.

Explosive behavior may occur when a person externalizes anxiety or anger. Sometimes, however, a person will internalize anxiety. A common way to internalize anxiety is to get sick. While the inmate may become explosive or aggressive, she may also manifest her anxiety by getting sick or becoming moody or depressed.

We can look at each scenario and think, "Gee, isn't that going a bit overboard, to get so mad?" Yet many of us have lashed out when confronted with the fear of loss of self-control. One place we can likely all relate to is the experience of the fear of loss of self-control while driving on the highway.

Fran's Bout with Road Rage

The Friday afternoon rush hour was intense as each driver raced home to start the weekend. A Subaru came up behind Fran's van, its high beams repeatedly flashing on and off, reflecting in Fran's mirror and on the back of his neck. Fran cursed at the driver behind him and called out, "Back off, you idiot!" Eventually, the gray Subaru pulled to the right of the van and slithered by while beeping its horn. It pulled up in front of the van. For the next two miles, Fran pulled up to less than one car length away from the small station wagon and screamed out, "Think you own the highway, ya moron?" and flashed his lights from low to high. "Ha, that'll teach ya," said Fran.

Fran felt powerful and in control as he chased down the other driver. A sense of satisfaction rushed through him as he thought, "I gave it to that son of a bitch."

Risking his own life and his passenger's, Fran responded in a way that is typical of a harried driver. The phenomenon is called "road rage." Too many accidents and deaths have occurred when drivers have become territorial and confrontational on the road. At one time or another, many of us have been in Fran's position. Responding to the fear of loss of self-control, we have allowed our emotions to govern our actions. Unbeknownst to Fran, however, the situation actually offered an opportunity to assume total control and transcend road rage. He could have let the Subaru pass and chosen not to be offended by the other driver's urgency. Instead, he felt challenged and threatened and did not see that he would have been both safe and in control had he just pulled over and let the Subaru pass. "Go ahead, friend. Travel safely," he could have thought.

Ten Tips for Re-directing Conflict

When an intervention goes well, I feel safe and those involved feel safe enough to listen to my suggestions. The following Ten Tips for Re-directing Conflict invite you, the reader, to simplify your intervention style while helping those involved in the conflict regain a sense of well-being and self-control.

Ten Tips for Re-directing Conflict	
1. Say a Lot by Saying a Little	6. Be Mindful of Words that Incite
2. Silence	7. Actively Listen
3. Acknowledge Emotions	8. Avoid Objectifying Yourself
4. Take One Step at a Time	9. Tell It Like It Is
5. Set the Pace	10. Create Opportunities

1. Say a Lot by Saying a Little

Mrs. Lewis and Matt

Mrs. Lewis walked into the front door of Pine Street High School and headed to the main office. After grabbing a cup of coffee and picking up her mail, she walked to her classroom and found Matt Simon, one of her senior students, standing at her door. "Mrs. Lewis," Matt said "I can't get no D in this class, you know. If I don't get at least a C—Man! I am so sick and tired of this stupid place. I can't get a D! Understand?" Mrs. Lewis replied…

What should Mrs. Lewis say to Matt? Let's review different statements for Mrs. Lewis and see how less can be more.

- "Good morning, Matt."

  This statement sets a norm that says, "I, Mrs. Lewis, am not upset by your swearing and demanding words" and is a civil acknowledgment of Matt that maintains neutrality.

- "Let me put down this mail, and we can talk about what is bothering you."

  The reply is a bit wordy and draws Mrs. Lewis right into the content. Asking an upset person to wait a minute while you put down your mail is likely to get him even more agitated. It is obvious that Matt has been waiting a while and wants some type of answer right then.

- "Would you like to step inside the room and speak with me?"

  This response is potentially dangerous. It is safer for the teacher and student to stay in the hallway, at least until Mrs. Lewis catches the attention of another teacher in the hallway. She might nod to the teacher and get some acknowledgment back, ensuring that she and Matt are being monitored.

- "You'd better lower your voice, young man!"

  This may get Matt to lower his voice, but it also may incite Matt to increase his volume. Matt may very well be expecting to hear something like "Lower your voice, young man," just so that he can continue to target Mrs. Lewis. "This is a low voice. You don't want to hear me get loud, lady," he might say.

- "I understand that getting a low mark can be pretty disappointing."

  Oops. Mrs. Lewis is forgetting to drop the content, before securing safety. In addition, I consider this response an interpretive statement. Another way of expressing compassion and integrating the third tip "acknowledging emotions" is to reflect the other person's feeling, as in, "You have a lot going on."

- "Glad you came to see me, Matt."

  This short statement speaks to Matt's need to be heard and begins the conversation on a positive note. By complimenting Matt's action, Mrs. Lewis takes the first step toward creating a working relationship with this troubled student. By the way, Matt is doing exactly what we would want any trouble student to do—seek out assistance from an adult. He may not be presenting himself in an exemplary manner, but at least he is trying.

Of all the responses, the first "Good morning, Matt" and "I'm glad you came to see me, Matt" are good examples of how to say a lot by saying a little. Feeling caught off guard or tongue-twisted during a conflict contributes to wordy replies. Participants get to experience this effect first hand while performing in a workshop role play, which I use to provide real time data for assessing our intervention styles.

Participants are directed to make up their own role plays, based upon real life experiences. The first time they do the role play, they are directed to allow the incident to escalate. This escalation is done because at times people in the audience will gasp and say, "I saw someone do the same thing yesterday. No wonder that scene escalated." When the same players do the role play a second time, there is a baseline from which we can decipher the correct way to help a person in conflict. The following role play illustrates two possible interventions for a secretary at a doctor's office who is managing an agitated patient.

Mr. Woodruff's Role Play

Mr. Woodruff was tapping his foot on the floor and looking at his watch for the umpteenth time in Dr. Harvey's waiting room. Dr. Harvey's secretaries Joan Sutherland and Marsha Pickett had barely noticed Mr. Woodruff's irritation. However, they were fully aware that the doctor's schedule was off by about an hour.

Mr. Woodruff got up from his seat and stomped over to Joan Sunderland's desk behind a glass window in the reception area.

Joan looked up.

"I want to see the doctor now!" Mr. Woodruff said, "I have been waiting for over an hour. My wife is at home waiting

for me, and she needs me to help her get around. I can't wait any longer."

"Well, would you like to reschedule?" Joan began.

"That's not what I want, and you know it," replied Mr. Woodruff.

Marsha Pickett, Joan's coworker, overheard the conversation and added her two cents. "This is a doctor's office. Now you pipe down! We will call you when it is your turn. Now either take a seat or please leave the waiting room."

"How dare you!" screamed Mr. Woodruff.

The conflict had begun to escalate. I stopped the role play and asked the man playing Mr. Woodruff, "What did you hear the secretaries say to you?"

"I didn't hear anything. I could feel that I was going to have to wait longer, and I felt pretty upset about that."

When I asked him what he wanted to hear, he replied, "I was hoping they would help me somehow."

The scene was to be replayed a second time with the secretaries practicing the first principle—say a lot by saying a little—while working toward the goal of helping Mr. Woodruff to regain a sense of well-being.

They began where Mr. Woodruff got up from his seat and stomped over to Joan Sunderland's reception area.

Joan Sunderland and Mr. Woodruff role play – Take 2

"I want to see the doctor now!" Mr. Woodruff said. "I have been waiting for over an hour. My wife is at home waiting for me and she needs me to help her get around. I can't wait any longer."

"Well, would you like to reschedule?" Joan Sunderland began.

"I need to see the doctor now," screamed Mr. Woodruff.

Marsha Pickett, whose desk was next to Joan Sunderland's, said, "Mr. Woodruff—"

Upon hearing his name, Mr. Woodruff turned his head in her direction and nodded.

"Let me help you over here."

"I want to see the doctor now," Mr. Woodruff said firmly but in a lower tone of voice.

"You have been very inconvenienced, and I am so sorry. The doctor had an emergency this morning, and it has set our office back. You see that woman over there? She is going in right now, and then it will be your turn. Would it help if you called your wife to check in on her?"

"Uh? Yeah. That would be good," he replied.

"Come over to my desk, and you can use this line."

The role play ended, and I asked Mr. Woodruff what he was able to hear this time around. He was able to recall specific examples such as "I heard my name" or "I heard that I was going to be helped."

When people are agitated, it is difficult for them to take in more than a few words from those who are trying to help. If you are the intervener, try using only short sentences—one to four worded interventions. Identify yourself and call the agitated person by name. If he is able to acknowledge the contact, he might be able to hear the next intervention. If he does not respond, it may be an indication of a psychotic state of mind, the use of drugs or alcohol, rage, or pure obstinacy. For the brief moment when an agitated person does respond to his name, a connection has been made and the beginnings of an alliance created. The person intervening can continue by acknowledging the alliance: "Thanks for listening" or "I appreciate your attentiveness."

If an agitated person responds to her name by a turn of the head, eye contact, or a gesture such as putting up her hand as if to say, "Don't bother me," the intervener can continue giving brief directives. "Turn away," "Come with me," or "Walk with me" are a few examples. The idea is to give clear verbal directives that can be heard and understood. More importantly, the directive should be concrete, attainable, and something she can physically do.

2. Silence

From experience, I know that it can be hard to keep quiet, especially when you feel that the other person is in the wrong. Most of us are used to uninhibited, rapid discourse with colleagues, friends, or family. It is challenging to hold back spontaneous reaction. A few seconds of attentive silence can feel like a lifetime during an intervention. However, presenting quiet composure saves time and keeps the intervention focused on safety. Resolution and debriefing can wait until all parties are willing to listen.

Practicing Silence

Quiet time alone at least once a day without the television or radio blaring may seem like a small request, but for many it can be difficult to achieve. In our society, we are used to constant multi-media stimulation. Try muting the television or putting on a music-only radio station or recording. Taking little steps makes the goal of being at peace with silence manageable and attainable.

Despite persistent attempts to get us riled, I believe a person in crisis is hoping that those who intervene will remain in control. Being comfortable with silence projects authority and ability.

3. Acknowledge Emotions

Providing an outlet and emotional space for someone who is holding tightly to his emotions is a small gesture that can guide him into a deeper understanding of how feelings affect actions. You can say, "This must be very hard for you to hear" or "Your lip is quivering. Do you want to cry?" Such leading statements permit the release of emotions. When people are upset or angry, they are vulnerable and can be led into an emotional release more easily than when they have regained their composure.

Some people cry, some yell, and others shake when upset. Holding back and not releasing your emotions only serves to increase the stress associated with a crisis. Letting out an emotional release in a safe setting, with a friend, a professional intervener, or a counselor can reduce tension and provide a renewed state of self-control.

Permission to Cry

> *Late one evening, I was called into the emergency room to see a patient who had been described on the phone to me by the nurse as catatonic. I was working as an on-call crisis intervener for the community human resource center. Not even his family had been able to get any response out of the man. Right after I arrived, he rose and walked out of the hospital. I followed him with an officer in a cruiser nearby to make sure the scene stayed safe. If the patient had become combative, or if he had threatened me verbally or physically, the officer could have exited the cruiser and spoken to the man. If necessary, he could have physically controlled the man to keep him safe and me out of harm's way. Fortunately neither concern occurred.*
>
> *The patient's face was grim and his body held stiffly. Walking by his side, I instinctively asked, "May I put my hand on your shoulder?"*
>
> *He nodded his head and began to cry. Once he was able to experience the emotional release, he told me how frustrated he was with having to do his taxes. It was April 14, the night before his tax return was due. He admitted to being overtired, frustrated, and stressed. I listened for a long time. After emoting, he was able to head home and return to his*

family. He needed some sleep and was able to decide it wasn't such a big deal to file an extension and do his return when he was under less stress.

Such emotional release can help people regain self-control. This man, lip quivering and body rigid, was able to reveal his vulnerability with a safe witness. Given the opportunity, people in pain will receive acts of kindness and release pent-up frustration and stress.

4. Take One Step at a Time

People in crisis can be consumed by the quest to find a solution to their situation. While the intervener is working towards safety, the parties in conflict are thinking, "How am I going to solve this problem right now?"

The tendency is for people in a state of emotional upheaval to take on more than they can handle. You can help initiate structure by directing the person to "take one step at a time." The first step is always aimed at helping the person regain a sense of self-control. Guiding the person to slow down his or her breathing, such as by saying, "Let's both take a deep breath in and out, slowly" or offering the person a glass of water, provides an immediate focus.

During crisis calls over the telephone, I first ask the person to take a seat. Once done, we have our first success. Then I ask them what he had to eat that day. This question can serve both to distract and to gather information about how well he is taking care of himself. You might also have the person find some crackers and take a few bites while on the phone. Remember that lack of food or high levels of alcohol can contribute to irrational or agitated behavior.

Once a person's physical well-being is addressed, you can begin to identify external factors that will continue to help him regain a sense of self-control. Notice how the statement, "Let's figure out what you can do right now, instead of what you have to do tonight" establishes focus on the immediate scene. As the intervener, you are like a gatekeeper. If you don't maintain a boundary around what should or shouldn't be discussed, then you will have an onslaught of information to manage.

Keeping the Moment in Perspective

> *During one late-night crisis phone call, I was talking with a woman who was so angry at her husband that she was ready to pack up her clothes and leave with the children. Knowing her history, I was aware that it was not a case of domestic violence. The couple had ongoing miscommunication, which often grew into threats about divorce and custody. She wanted to talk about how she was going to leave and get a divorce. I asked her instead what she could do right now that would help her and her children get some sleep. When she started to take smaller steps and not discuss what she was going to do with the rest of her life, the problem became more manageable and she regained her self-control.*

I knew that determining a long-term solution to the woman's conflict with her husband should occur when she was not as emotionally reactive or angry. Once the initial volatility of the conflict had diminished and she had regained a sense of self-control, she might be referred to seek individual counseling, couples counseling, or professional mediation services to discuss plans for the rest of her life.

Leading into Present Time

Directing a person to stay in "present time" is a manageable goal. What he can do immediately, while you are speaking to him, helps to break down what feels like an insurmountable crisis. For the woman on the phone, present time meant leaving her husband in the living room and going into her bedroom to talk with me. I instructed her to get a glass of water and take a few slow breaths. She did so and immediately felt more in control of her emotions. From this new starting point, we were able to discuss that the children needed to take baths and get tucked into bed. She didn't have to speak to her husband, she decided, and she agreed that if she did, she would only get upset again.

Sometimes the person in crisis can figure out what steps are needed to provide immediate relief. The woman that I was speaking with needed to be advised. She was too upset to think clearly. Setting up tangible, incremental steps helps those in crisis succeed immediately.

5. Set the Pace

Avoid matching an angry person's level of agitation. You may hear, "Everyone says they want to help, but no one ever does," or "Okay. Are you going to do this for me or what? Come on, hurry up!" You can create an alliance by saying, "I want to help. Will you work with me to make it happen?" The intervener must set the pace. Stating, "You are speaking quickly. Please slow down. I want to hear" is a concrete, physical request that a person can do immediately, and, it sets the pace.

If a person gets agitated again because you are not going fast enough to meet her needs, remember that your objective is to keep the scene safe and to take one step at a time. A person who feels that nothing and no one is helping him will not be helped by others who match his frenetic energy. Back up your request, by saying "What you're saying is important." If they then do indeed slow down, thank them. "Good job. I appreciate you working with me."

The conflict management leader has to maintain self-control. An angry person will take notice of a quiet and professional demeanor and will often follow suit. Whether it is a medical emergency or an emotional crisis, the person in charge is expected to be level-headed and confident. An angry person is also not used to receiving a compliment. Well-timed compliments, if sincere, can provide a mutual pause to the moment, and set the pace.

6. Be Mindful of Words that Incite

One of the most overused phrases that can immediately incite is to tell a person to "Calm down!" Not only is this statement commanding and patronizing, it is often ineffective.

"Calm what?"

"My actions?"

"My words?"

"My voice?"

Instead, tell people exactly what they are doing, such as, "You're talking fast." Providing clear information about what people in crisis are or are not doing gives them something tangible to work with:

"You are breathing really quickly."

"You're pacing quickly. Please slow down, so I can hear you."

Terms like "Stop acting out!" "Relax!" or "Get a grip!" mean little to a person in crisis. Think. What is it that is not calm about the person? Is it their movements, rapid speech, or tone? Be concrete.

"You're talking really fast."

"Please slow down."

Pause.

Then repeat the phrase again.

If the person acknowledges you by slowing his speech, you can say, "Thanks for listening." If instead, he get angry and says, "Stop saying that!" you know that at least he heard you. Move on to your next one-liner. "Sure. I'm taking a step back." This last statement provides a bit of physical distance and is very descriptive.

Follow these statements with:

"I'm going to take a slow breath in."

They can join you or not. Avoid saying, "You need to take a breath." Such a statement is condescending.

Leading a person toward behaviors that provide instant relief and control is very different from demanding that he act in a manner that makes you comfortable. If the person resists your request, avoid feeling offended. Remain in control of your emotions. Perhaps silence is required for a moment or two. Constant awareness of personal safety and scene safety is definitely required. Securing scene safety may require you to stand back and give the person in crisis breathing room to move around without causing personal harm or harm to others.

Sometimes people are unresponsive to attempts geared toward helping them regain a sense of self-control. Intoxicated people are less inclined to listen. When someone is intoxicated and acting in a dangerous way, perhaps threatening others, the person should be given a lot of room to move around. As a last resort, someone intoxicated may be physically restrained and put into mechanical restraints, like handcuffs. Not just anyone can detain a person. Police officers are given authorization to use such devices. Nonprofessionals should not place other people in mechanical restraint. You could severely injure a person by tying them up and compromising their circulation or ability to breathe. There are so many other choices available before you need to consider resorting to physical management—this is true for professional and nonprofessional interveners.

Crisis intervention requires you to find your own style so that you gain confidence in your skills. Try practicing the exact words you might use. I have integrated the short phrases introduced in this book into my interventions. You may wish to use a variation of these phrases to suit your own style and personality.

7. Actively Listen

As a communication skill, active listening is invaluable, whether you are managing a conflict or consoling a friend. People like to know that they are being heard. Application of this technique requires attentive listening skills like nodding and maintaining alert eye contact. Encouraging statements such as, "Could you say more?" or "Please go on," or "Take your time. I want to hear what you are saying" let the other person know that she is heard and also provide an opportunity for her to elaborate. In an earlier example, Luke used active listening skills with Mary to find out what was troubling her. Mary said, "I'm so mad." Luke provided a lead-in to further discussion without being too wordy: "Say more."

His two words implied, "I would like to hear all about what happened, Mary," a wordy statement that was shortened with a simple "Say more."

Escalation occurs when someone feels threatened and shut down. You may inadvertently shut a person down by being long-winded or saying, with a sharp tone, "Speak up. I can't hear you" or "Look at me when I am talking with you" or "Are you sure that is what happened?" or "Is that all you have to say for yourself?"

Once a person feels threatened, he will focus on the threat, rendering him unable to hear anything else. With that said, it is worth the effort to take a more expansive view on the definition of active listening. Listen not only to what the other person is saying but also to your own tone and choice of words.

8. Avoid Objectifying Yourself

You objectify yourself when you make interventions like, "The rules are..." or "The program says that..." or "In this house we..."

A program's philosophy or the house rules of a family home provide parameters that govern the way people are expected to interact with each other. Rules are easy targets because rules have no feelings or personality. A statement like "I hate the rules" is not a personal attack at any one person. A rule can be called every nasty name possible and will never be impacted by such name-calling. People, though, can be triggered by name-calling and verbal attacks.

Instead of making a rule statement, try to humanize the intervention by saying, "When I found the dirty dishes in the sink, I felt angry and upset." The receiver of your statement might still say, "I hate you, and I don't care how you feel," but that same person will have to face the repercussion of a nasty response. You might respond to the disagreeable response by getting angry, by looking down or away, or by becoming sad and hurt. The visual impact of seeing that you have been affected by what was said has a greater potential for making an attacker think twice about such direct, malicious statements.

Let us look at two different types of corrective statements made by a teacher to a student who is swearing in a classroom. The first example illustrates an impersonalized approach by the teacher.

Example 1

"You know the rules. No swearing."

Such a straightforward intervention might stop the student, but it is more likely that he or she will continue to test the boundaries of the classroom. A more personalized intervention would be using what is called an "I statement."

Example 2

"I treat you with respect. Please don't swear at me."

Maybe this is too formal for your style. You might want to use a different choice of words. I know that sometimes I do sound a bit corny, even—gasp—old fashion, but it has been my experience that such statements catch a person's attention.

What counts is that the request be authentic. People in crisis can spot a phony, insincere request a mile away.

Reference to rules of a program or the "house rules" are best discussed when the person is able and willing to reason with the intervener—post crisis. Reminders about the rules should not be done when a person is highly agitated and looking for a target on which to vent her anger. Humanize your intervention by saying, "What you are saying feels mean-spirited," or "I am here to help."

Working with a Shoplifter

> *I had a job for a season working at an outdoor clothing store when I was in my twenties. The store was in New Haven, Connecticut, and had a storefront facing out toward a busy sidewalk and main thoroughfare in the city. One day, a young man walked in and took a couple of expensive rain jackets into the dressing room. I had a gut feeling that something wasn't right because of his gruff manner. I called the manager, who came in and waited with me for the man to come out of the dressing room. We both saw immediately that the rain jackets had been stuffed under the patron's own coat that he was wearing. "Hey, you. This store prosecutes shoplifters," the manager called out to the young man. The manager then said to me, "Call the police." In the next moment, I saw the young man push the manager over into a clothing rack and head out the door. He was gone in a flash, and the manager was pretty shaken up.*

By stating, "This store prosecutes shoplifters," the manager had set himself up to become a target. Interestingly, I had been standing right next to the manager, but had not been pushed by the young man. He could have pushed me, too, but his focus was on the manager who had become the alienating establishment.

I learned a big lesson that day and knew that I would avoid putting myself in the same situation. Another time, I happened to see another person shoplifting at the same store. I walked up to the girl and said, "I make four dollars and twenty five cents an hour. That shirt you have in your bag is going to set me back a whole day's worth of wages." I recall that the shoplifter looked at me with wide eyes. For a moment, we looked into each other's eyes. Then she reached into her bag, passed me the shirt, and hurried out of the store.

At no time during the intervention did I become "The Store". By speaking about how her actions would impact me directly, I avoided becoming a target and instead made an ally. My statement was certainly heartfelt because I was held accountable for my inventory. Regardless of whether or not I would have to pay the store for her theft wasn't the point. I wasn't going to get into a wrestling match over a shirt after seeing the manager get shoved by the last person caught stealing in the store. Personal safety was my priority, but the least I could do then was to let her know that someone other than the store would be affected by her theft. Her change of heart became a win/win situation for the two of us.

9. Tell It Like It Is

It is a natural tendency for humans to strive to understand the significance of another's behavior. Such an analytical approach, though, can cause you to overlook the obvious. The following example illustrates this point.

Redirecting Darren's Threat

A workshop participant asked to review an intervention she had with a client.

"I was in my office meeting with Darren, who was acting as if everyone in the building were at fault for his problems. I was left speechless when he said, "You people drive me crazy. You, you are always nagging me. You remind me of my aunt. I feel like smacking you in the face."

I asked the workshop participant what she said to Darren.

"I said, 'What is it about me that reminds you of your aunt?'"

She told us that Darren started to tell her all the ways that she, his aunt, and his mother had made life miserable for him. She said she felt safe only when a supervisor came into the office and was able to distract Darren.

This intervener was looking at every possible reason why Darren had made the threat. "Hmm," she seemed to have thought, "Maybe he had some prior problems with his aunt. How can I look like his aunt? We are not the same age." I told her to take what Darren had said at face value and give him a direct reply.

"I am not your aunt, and I do not want you to hit me."

Stating that you do not want someone to hit you may sound like a weak statement. But stating directly that you do not want to be hit is different from quivering and pleading not to be hit.

When I asked the rest of the workshop participants what was the one thing they all thought when they heard Darren say that he wanted to hit this woman, they all agreed that they were thinking, "Gee, I hope he doesn't hit her." If it had been they that Darren had threatened, they also would have feared for their own safety.

In other words, when faced with a bizarre statement, don't overanalyze. Take it at face value. Decide what it is that you do or don't want an agitated person to do, and then state your side. You can also follow through by saying, "I am here to help you. Let's talk about ways we can work together." Such a statement forms a working alliance, which an intervener and a person in crisis can use to move on from the bizarre comment.

Darren had made a very real threat. When the worker did not call him on it, she was overlooking an important indicator of potential danger.

10. Create Opportunities

When I think about creating opportunities, I think about a world event that demonstrated a peaceful resolution to an ongoing conflict: the fall of the Berlin Wall that had separated East Germany from West Germany from 1961 to 1989. Like many people who had grown up during the Cold War, I never expected the Berlin Wall would be taken down. I certainly did not expect the wall to come down in the peaceful, celebratory way that it did beginning on November 9, 1989. Miracles do happen, given the opportunity.

Not anticipating the possibility of positive change can result in unimpressive outcomes or, worse, self-fulfilling prophecies. Statements like, "That child has been kicked out of every school system in the country. I wish you a lot of luck come September. You are going to need it" or "Dad is never going to change. He never listens to my side of the story and he never will," perpetuate a sense of failure for all. When a person hears statements about himself like, "Here comes trouble with a capital T," being "bad" becomes part of his persona regardless of his present behavior. Changing a reputation is hard enough to do, but it becomes nearly impossible when everyone surrounding him expects failure. Instead, create an opportunity for a ray of hope that people can change for the better.

Being non-judgmental and optimistic does not mean that you are a pushover. On the contrary, such traits are proactive. Believing in a person's potential despite her history is a trait of an effective intervener. Healing and change do happen, given the opportunity.

Redirecting Michael toward a New Goal

Michael was young, fearless, and obstinate toward authority. He was in a short-term treatment setting where I was a staff member. Michael seemed to have an unwavering goal to get me angry or embarrass me. I was sure he spent every waking hour thinking of ways to get me upset.

Instead of correcting him, I decided to do exactly what he didn't expect. I leveled with him—in other words I told him like it is. I asked him into my office and told him that he was doing a great job of getting me going, day in and day out. We could continue like this until he left the program, I told him, but I had a job to do. I said, "I think you are smarter than that, and I'm hoping that you are wanting to wave good-bye to this place and are going to become a positive leader for this group. You are a natural leader, but you have to choose which way you are going to go. You can waste your time here or you can take control of your life."

Michael looked dumbfounded and didn't reply. Later that day, though, I noticed that Michael had changed. He began speaking up to other group members who were horse-playing and disrespecting staff. I vividly recall breathing a sigh of relief, both for Michael and myself. He had certainly been "getting my goat," an exhausting experience that benefits no one.

I also made an important change that morning by embracing the concept of "create opportunities." It is hard to keep the faith when you have to manage angry and aggressive people. It is easy to become cynical, consumed, and emotionally depleted. Our conflict changed the moment I chose to reorient my judgment of Michael. Instead of seeing him as a nuisance, I was able to rise above that limited view and offer the opportunity for him to channel his behavior in a way that rewarded him. Aggression can be reshaped into the positive attribute of assertion, if you provide appropriate direction and leadership.

Summary

Refining your technique and trying new approaches is scary and takes courage. Be patient with yourself. You can transform what appears to be a complex problem into a simple, step-by-step conflict management procedure. Once personal safety is secured, multiple options for redirecting conflict will come to light. The Ten Tips for Redirecting Conflict provide a resource of options for addressing the conflict management goal of helping those in conflict regain a sense of self-control. Instead of feeling overwhelmed by conflict, you become enticed to create opportunities for change.

Don't Forget to Breathe

There is a sound of ah-ing in the woods. You hear it and know a storm is nigh, and every tree knows it, and every waving branch.

— John Muir

In the snow-laden hills of western Massachusetts, in the mountains of British Columbia, and surrounded by the eucalyptus forest of Santa Cruz, I have breathed deeply. And I have never forgotten the smell of the fragrant air in each place.

In my yard, surrounding the driveway, stand tall Eastern White Pines. Even the subtlest wind will make the trees sing "Whoosh!" Having lived in a forest landscape for some time now, I have come to rely on the pines each time I come home from a business trip or long day away. The formidable trees sway above me, enticing me to sigh and breathe in.

This chapter explores the effect and influence of breath throughout an intervention. Although we all breathe, not all of us exercise the full potential of purposeful breathing during an intervention.

The involuntary nature of the respiratory system allows us to work, play, and sleep without having to give a thought to breathing. In each twenty-four hour cycle, a healthy adult takes approximately seventeen thousand breaths. Breathing happens, even if we choose temporarily to hold our breath, slow it down, or quicken the rate.

The respiratory system is paradoxical. There is an apparent contradiction in the ability to be voluntary and involuntary at the same time. I remember my childhood effort to test this contradiction, holding my breath until my involuntary system took over, forcing me to exhale with a loud puff. My innocent, analytical mind was both challenged and perplexed by this physiological enigma.

Martial arts, the practice of yoga, and many exercise programs teach breathing techniques. Professional athletes use breathing as a way of maintaining focus while staying relaxed. Notice the basketball player preparing to take a foul shot, the pitcher readying for a throw, the football player gearing up for the kick. They set their stance, take a moment to pause, and then breathe to focus the moment. Deliberate use of breathing techniques elevates breathing from an automatic function to a meditative form of self-control. Managing our breathing during a crisis and helping others regain control of respiration are part of the crisis intervener's role.

How We Breathe

Our lungs extend from the top of the shoulders all the way down to the base of the rib cage. Breathing that expands the belly along with the chest is known as abdominal breathing. Quality abdominal breaths are deliberate, requiring slow intake and full expansion.

Short, gulping breathing that raises only the upper chest cavity is known as chest breathing. This type of breathing requires that the involuntary system take over when we need to expel carbon dioxide. The brain, which is the command center for vital functions, maintains bodily function by coordinating adequate oxygen intake and carbon dioxide expulsion. Through an occasional yawn or sigh, we relieve tension and expel carbon dioxide.

Emotions strongly influence the rate of respiration. In his book *Conscious Breathing* (1995), Gay Hendricks writes about the fight-or-flight response and how it affects our breathing: "Belly muscles tighten, our breath shifts up into the chest, and our breathing speeds up. We are poised to run or fight back." Hendricks also notes the capacity to take charge of our breathing: "Human consciousness is powerful enough that we can notice when we are in a stressed breathing pattern and do something about it. We can consciously take deeper, slower breaths, and we can consciously shift our breathing from chest to belly."

Lifeguarding and Breathing Dependence

I spent two of my college summers as a lifeguard at Indian Wells State Park on the Housatonic River in Connecticut. Sitting on a ten-foot tall, white chair, I was in full view of the entire beach. Whenever I stood up, blew the whistle, or jumped off my perch, it seemed that the entire waterfront would watch in anticipation of a rescue.

The general public expects lifeguards to perform their duties in an exemplary manner. I likely disappointed a few people on the beach when, running with a tank of oxygen over the sandy beach to the scene of a rescue, I stumbled and fell flat on the ground. I had no choice except to get myself up and keep running. But the wind had been knocked out of my lungs, and each step I took became a Herculean feat.

From behind me, as I moved slowly down the beach, I heard the familiar voice of one of my lifeguard team members say, "I'll take the tank." I quickly passed the oxygen to him and off he ran. I stood for a moment and slowed down my breathing. Once my breathing slowed, I was able to set off running with little effort. At the scene, I found that my team members had quickly rescued the swimmer. He was sitting on the beach upon one of our wool blankets and breathing normally. I thanked the guard who had taken the tank for helping me out and then headed back to my post.

When performing a rescue, a lifeguard's oxygen supply is vulnerable and is never to be taken for granted. A drowning swimmer is desperate and hysterical. Given the chance, he will flail at, climb upon, and push a rescuer underwater. Water rescuers are an extreme illustration of crisis interveners who are necessarily acutely aware of the importance of maintaining a steady flow of oxygen. However, when it comes to needing oxygen to function, the human brain doesn't differentiate between full-time professional and nonprofessional emergency workers.

Direct care staff, teachers, nurses, parents, and other non-aquatic conflict managers frequently disregard breathing techniques as superfluous when managing a crisis. "I want to know what to say. I don't have time to think about my breathing" is a common statement by participants of my crisis intervention seminars. "Breathing is, after all, second nature."

Given that so many groups I have worked with consider breathing control to be unimportant, I started to facilitate a structured exercise focusing on breath. Participants are asked to stand up and then state their name and job title. As we go around the room, the pace quickens. Instead of waiting to stand and then speak, most participants introduce themselves while they are rising out of their chair. Some people's voices are shaky, and other people look flushed. They often speak so rapidly that it is hard to hear exactly what they are saying.

Although everyone knows exactly "what to say," most flounder during the mini-crisis commonly known as "The Fear of Public Speaking." Most speakers look nervous and fail to project confidence.

To help practice maintaining self-control and their rate of respiration, I ask the group members to try the same exercise again. This time, I direct them to stand and focus on their breathing by exhaling before saying a word. Once again, a few people begin speaking before they have stood upright. Overall, though, each person is more in command of himself. Instead of stumbling over words or rushing to finish, participants take their time and speak in an even cadence. Rather than feeling embarrassed for the uncomfortable speakers, the audience is able to relax and really listen.

Like any audience, people in crisis are sensitive to what key players are projecting. They will quickly lose confidence and may even provoke interveners who fail to maintain professional composure during a conflict. What we convey through our stance is often more defining than our words. A normal rate of respiration using abdominal breathing relaxes the body. Besides relaxing the body, purposeful breathing enhances the brain's capacity for critical decision making and problem solving. Seminar participants appear stiff and nervous when they don't take time to focus on their breathing. Interveners who employ breathing techniques find themselves in an open posture that is conducive to creating an alliance with those in conflict.

Breathing as an Indicator

A person in crisis also needs to regain a normal rate of respiration. Agitation, breath holding, and speaking quickly suppress the supply of oxygen. Such a stressed state compromises people's ability to hear even the most effective interventions. The following vignette illustrates how an intervener who fails to notice a breathing indicator has difficulty helping a person in crisis regain self-control.

Ken Jones

> *Ken Jones scowled, and his chest was heaving up and down. He had just been sent to the office of the high school vice-principal, Jane Crown, after his homeroom teacher had found him in the hallway arguing with his girlfriend. "Mister Jones," Mrs. Crown began, "this is twice in one week that you have made an appearance in my office. This is not going to look good on your record this term, and I do plan on speaking with your parents. I knew your older sister, Kimberly, who was the valedictorian of her class. Mister Jones, are you listening to me?"*
>
> *Ken was staring out the window behind Mrs. Crown. "Mister Jones!" Mrs. Crown repeated. He looked up at her. "Did you hear one word that I just said?" demanded Mrs. Crown.*

Ken looked blankly at the vice-principal and said, "What?"

The vice-principal's intervention is a classic example of an intervener who unknowingly sabotages her own intervention. A short and concise statement is best when speaking to an agitated person. Mrs. Crown's long-winded lecture was too much for Ken to hear. Her reference to Ken's sister Kimberly was self-serving and only complicated her intervention.

Let's give Mrs. Crown another chance. This time, she will be more attentive to Ken's fidgeting and his abnormally heavy breathing.

Ken Jones Take – 2

Ken Jones scowled, and his chest was heaving up and down. He had just been sent to the office of the high school vice-principal, Jane Crown, after his homeroom teacher had found him in the hallway arguing with his girlfriend. "Ken," Mrs. Crown began, "you're breathing fast!" The vice-principal then took a purposefully loud inhale and slowly exhaled. "Slooow breaths," she said in a low voice. Ken shook his head a bit and turned to look at her. "That's it. Let's work on our breathing first. Okay?" She had clearly caught Ken's attention. He was looking at her in a quizzical manner while breathing deeply through his nose. "Easy, buddy." she said. "Our breath can be a good friend when the world feels like it is spinning way too fast."

Conflict management is all about focusing in on a single moment. Mrs. Crown concentrated on Ken's breathing pattern, which is exactly what he needed in order to regain a sense of self-control. "One to Four Worded Interventions" are easier for a person in distress to hear rather than long, drawn out statements. Short phrases like, "breathing fast" don't need to be grammatically correct. As Mrs. Crown began to feel that Ken was becoming calmer, her statements grew longer but stayed on task. Her compassionate style of gently guiding the student toward a normal rate of respiration was conducive to building a connection with Ken. He might still be unwilling to discuss the details of his dispute with his girlfriend; but regardless, Mrs. Crown has demonstrated and led Ken through an important exercise that he might be able to use again on his own.

The vice-principal would now be able to discuss the importance of breathing and its use during conflict. The following dialogue might direct Ken to rethink how he manages conflict.

> *"Ken, when you came into this office you were breathing so fast, you couldn't hear one word that I was saying. Remember?"*

Whether or not the student agrees verbally with a "yes, I remember" or with a nod of the head is unimportant. As long as he is breathing normally, her words would be heard. Pushing him to agree with the obvious, that yes, indeed, he was breathing fast and couldn't hear one word she was saying, would only serve to distract him from the overall lesson of this meeting. For instance, he might think, "If I agree to this statement, does it mean I am agreeing that I should be punished for my behavior or that I was in the wrong?" Until he was able to get a sense of where the vice-principal was going with her line of reasoning, Ken might wait for her full statement before agreeing to anything. She would need to continue with something like,

> *"Ken, I have learned that if a person isn't breathing normally, he will have a hard time focusing on what another person is saying. I made a couple of statements that helped you refocus on your breathing. What might you be able to do next time you are in a heated argument with another person? Or, how could you help someone who is upset and breathing rapidly?"*

Mrs. Crown could now wait for a likely reply, since the student isn't being berated for his behavior. Additionally, Ken has been empowered to share his insight on how to help another person. If Ken replies with, "I can help them slow down their breathing" or "Breathe," the vice-principal could then lead the conversation toward discussing the dispute he had been engaged in before he was sent to the office. Not only would Mrs. Crown have created an alliance: she has guided Ken to think for himself and shown him that she valued his thoughts on such matters.

Even if Ken refuses to reply to her request, he would now be in control of his breathing. Whether he wants to acknowledge that his slowed breathing pattern was better than his prior breathing would not make or break this intervention. As long as the person in crisis has regained some semblance of self-control, the primary goal has been achieved. Expecting a person to become conversational is too high of an expectation for some. It takes time to build trust. Nevertheless, Mrs. Crown has achieved a small victory. She could follow up with Ken again and meet with him to show concern for his well-being and acknowledge just how well he could do something when he sets his mind to the task.

A Proactive Intervener—John F. Stephen

I was twenty-one years old and had no direct care experience when I first started working at Long Lane School. Luckily, I was assigned to work with John F. Stephen, a man who had both experience and an innate ability to thwart conflicts before they became unmanageable.

John was proactive in his intervention style. His continual observations kept him one step ahead of the group. I enjoyed watching him greet clients as they entered the room for group session. He didn't say something to everyone, but if he saw someone who looked pensive and distracted, he might say something off the cuff and nonsensical, like "Do you like orange juice?" or "Purple Haze." Usually, the client would make some reply by giggling, pulling back, or smirking. John just stood there cool as a cucumber, with eyes on the client and an ever-present toothpick held to one side of his mouth.

When a person responded to John by saying, "What are you talking about, man?" John would reply, "Glad you could make it today."

As I watched the clients John had singled out enter the room and take a seat, I noticed that two things occurred. They would look around to see if anyone had noticed their interaction with John, and then their bodies would relax. The question served to distract clients and let them know that John had noticed them. John didn't wait until an individual had become immersed in anger. At the first sign of a client's discomfort-held breath, hunched shoulders, or eyes cast down, he made an intervention.

The ability to notice breathing as an indicator of one's emotional state requires a keen sense of how you breathe yourself. John's ever-present toothpick was part of his regime to quit smoking. It humanized him by demonstrating that he was familiar with stress. It seemed logical, therefore, that he had the ability to see it in others.

Training Yourself to See Breath as an Indicator

A fearful person might make a wheezing sound, hold his breath, or hyperventilate. Flared nostrils and forceful breathing are signs of frustration. Loud sighing or hisses are obvious indications of irritability or fear. By noticing variations in breathing and other outward indicators like clenched fists or a flushed and sweaty face, you can make a quick analysis of a person's probable state of mind.

Through observation, you can train yourself to see breathing as an indicator of emotion. There are many opportunities, from crowded express lines to family reunions, to observe how a person's breathing matches his physical or emotional state.

Next time you are waiting in the checkout line in the grocery store, watch the breathing patterns of the other patrons or the cashier. It might look something like the scenario described below.

Snorting in the Checkout Line

Holly and Tomas stopped at the supermarket to pick up some necessities. They were going to the 7:30 movie and knew that the store would be closed before the movie finished. It was 7:15; they had fifteen minutes to make it on time. They moved efficiently through the store. They were doing well until they reach the express line.

In front of them were Mrs. Harris and her two daughters, picking up a few extra items for their Sunday dinner with relatives. As Mrs. Harris and her family meandered up to the checkout and began putting their items meticulously on the conveyor belt, Holly and Tomas began shifting from one foot to another, both thinking, "We'll make it. She has only eight items."

But when Mrs. Harris took out her checkbook and slowly began writing in her elegant script, Tomas sighed. "How long does it take for someone to write a check?" he whispered loud enough for Holly, the cashier, and the rest of the customers in the line to hear. Holly looked up nervously at Tomas and then at the customers behind him who quickly shifted their eyes and looked away. Everyone held his breath except for Tomas, who was snorting like a bull while thinking about missing his favorite part, the coming attractions. When Mrs. Harris and her two girls finally completed their transaction, the line sighed in unison. Holly and Tomas shoved their items to the cashier, who hurriedly checked them out.

Tomas conveyed his dissatisfaction through his exaggerated breathing. Like a canine's growl, his breathing was powerful and impacted those around him.

A Withheld Breath at a Family Gathering

Lucille and her two sisters, Helen and Maggie, sat around the kitchen table after finishing the dishes and putting away the food from Thanksgiving dinner. A few other relatives sat with them, having coffee. The mood was light and conversation was easy. When Maggie began talking about the upcoming birth of her third grandchild, Helen got up and walked to the sink. Lucille, the oldest of the three sisters, knew that Helen had a hard time listening to the story since Helen's daughter and son-in-law had had too many miscarriages to mention. Lucille walked over to Helen and put her arm around her younger sister, who had barely taken in a breath of air since standing up. Maggie, realizing her mistake, let out a quiet sigh and slowly shook her head. Five-year-old Timothy Junior said loudly, "What's wrong, everybody?"

Even as children, we begin to notice changes in breathing that occur when family members have disagreements or share in the joy of birth or loss of a loved one. Learning to recognize breathing as an indicator of emotion isn't a new concept. We simply need to fine-tune old skills and use them during interventions.

Commanding Another to Exhale

Kate, on hall duty at the junior high, heard a loud and angry voice from the main stairwell and quickly headed in the direction of the noise. She saw two familiar students standing only a few feet apart. Jeff's nostrils flared, and his face was flushed. The other boy looked frightened and was cowering against the wall. Kate entered the large stairwell and saw clearly that Jeff was holding his air in, his chest puffed up. Aware of her own safety, she moved into Jeff's line of vision, about four feet away, and said, "Exhale, Jeff. Exhale!" Then she puffed up her cheeks and released an explosion of air. The air rushed from Jeff's nose and mouth. Before he could say anything, Kate said, "That's great, Jeff. Now, how about inhaling, too?"

Kate understood that in order to direct Jeff, she would first have to help him gain control of his breathing. It also caused a distraction, since "Exhale, Jeff. Exhale!" wasn't what Jeff expected anyone to say to him. When Kate exhaled, it was hard for Jeff not to join in, since he was holding his breath and his brain was likely begging for him to breathe again.

As a rule, you should be sure that the other person is capable of hearing the intervention. Irregular respiration is often due to a particular state of mind and as such can affect a person's ability to think clearly. As mentioned before, peripheral vision may be diminished. Instead of saying a lot of words to this person, you should lead him first into a more controlled breathing pattern. If a person regains a regular rhythm, he often becomes less agitated, and he may be able to manage the conflict on his own.

Here are two ways to lead a person back to a normal breathing pattern: Guided Breathing and Paced Breathing.

Guided Breathing

Guided breathing is like sharing a yawn. We have all experienced the chain reaction sparked by someone else's yawn. If I verbally draw attention to my breathing when intervening, the other person becomes aware of my respiration and is likely to attend to his own breathing. When I demonstrate a deep, slow breath, he may be inclined to follow along. During an intervention, it is just as important for the intervener as for the person in crisis to be breathing slowly and fully. Avoid saying, "You need to take a deep breath." Such a patronizing statement may only inspire resistance. A less confrontational approach would be to say, "Let's both take a deep breath." The person being spoken to has been respectfully offered a direction and the opportunity for control.

This technique can also be used with someone who is agitated and talking fast. You can say, "I want to hear you, but you are talking so fast that I can't. Let's both take a deep breath." If the person continues talking, the intervener can take a couple of slow, purposeful, deep breaths with the chest rising and falling each time. If the person asks, "What are you doing?" Your reply could be, "I am hoping you will slow your breathing, so we can work together."

Too Enticing to Refuse

> *In my early twenties, I had made an appointment with a naturopathic doctor to get information about some intense abdominal cramps I had recently experienced. A few days before, I had gone to the emergency room and was told that I might have an ulcer, although the ER doctor was not really certain and had recommended that I go see my regular doctor. As I walked into his office, the first thing he did was take a slim, glass carafe filled with crystal clear water from a rack. Attached to the rack was a clear, eight-ounce water glass. As he poured the pure, cool water from the carafe into the glass, my mouth began to water. He asked calmly, "So, how much water have you been drinking lately?"*
>
> *I nearly climbed across the desk for the glass. Though that happened over twenty years ago, I will never forget the power of his nonverbal suggestion. By the way, I did not have an ulcer. I was dehydrated.*

Like a fine glass of water, breathing is something to be savored. The doctor easily enticed me to drink more water. Similarly, you can encourage a person in crisis to become aware of his or her breathing by purposefully modeling deliberate inhalations and exhalations.

Paced Breathing

Try accelerating your breathing to the rapid pace of a person in crisis. Then, slowly decelerate your breathing. The person might look at you as if to say, "What is your problem?" It is both a reminder and a distraction to tell her, quite matter-offactly, that you are breathing at the same rate that she is. It encourages her to shift her focus to her respiration. A word of warning, though, with this technique: make sure you do not compromise your own composure by breathing too rapidly and thereby making yourself lightheaded and dizzy!

The following story illustrates another way of lowering the rate of respiration through a paced breathing count.

Helping Phyllis Regain Control of Her Breathing

> *On the morning of the training program called "Working with Survivors of Sexual Abuse," I noted that Phyllis was nervous by her continual shifting body and downward turned face. During the workshop, she was quiet and removed from the group discussions. When evaluations were being handed in, another participant asked me to see Phyllis, who was in the back room. She was trembling when I entered. I had a strong sense that in some way the workshop had triggered an emotional response for her. I offered my assistance. She said she couldn't drive home because she was so shaky.*
>
> *She allowed me to take her pulse. It was very rapid. Her breath was shallow and her face was red. I asked her to breathe with me for a minute. To a count of three, we both inhaled. We held our breath for a count of four and then breathed out for a count of three. I increased the count to five, then six. At the same time, I asked her to hold on to the table in front of us and feel the texture of the old oak. As Phyllis focused on her breathing and the tactile stimulation of the table, her trembling went away and her pulse rate decreased.*

The exercise that I used with Phyllis was tangible and accessible. At first she felt unable to control both her emotions and her body. By intentionally taking control of her respirations, she took the first step toward gaining back her self-control.

Asking her to hold on to the table brought Phyllis into "present time". This particular technique works well when counseling someone who is scared, angry, or delusional.

Having a concrete, tactile focus brings the person's thoughts to the present. You can use a table, the carpet, or the floor—anything physically concrete.

Counseling on the Phone

Crisis clinicians who counsel people over the phone use techniques like "present time" to help soothe a client. The clinician may ask the client to sit down and then describe the chair that she is sitting in. Is it wood, or is it upholstered? The clinician may then repeat the client's descriptive words, "You are sitting in your living room, in that comfy arm chair that you keep by the window."

Simple questions that a caller can answer provide attainable goals that are like stepping-stones across a stream. If the stones are too far apart, the caller may not attempt to cross. Evenly spaced stones, like accessible questions that provide the caller with instant success, can be used as a foundation for the rest of the conversation. For instance, if the person begins to get agitated while explaining the reason for the call, you could mention his emotional control displayed a moment ago.

Preliminary questions like finding out if he has eaten or taken medication also serve to provide important baseline information. When counseling a client, family member, or friend on the phone, the goal is to make sure that he feels safe from harm and is capable of taking care of himself. If he is unable to feed himself, he is clearly in need of a face-to-face interview or home visit and possible referral to a hospital. In-depth analysis should take place only in person.

Over the Phone Breathing Exercise

Once the initial introductory questions are completed, you can ask the person if she would like to do a breathing exercise. Before you start the exercise, ask the person to sit down. A seated position is more conducive to relaxation than standing.

Ask the person to try breathing in through the nose and out through the mouth and to do so while you count for them. This style of breathing helps a person in crisis control her inhalations and exhalations. If you fail to give directions on how to breathe, some people may do the entire exercise while breathing through their mouth. Mouth breathing leads to a shallower, gasping style of inhalation and exhalation and is not desirable.

Begin the exercise with,

"Inhale. One, one-thousand; two, one-thousand; three, one-thousand; four, one-thousand. And hold your breath. One, one-thousand; two, one-thousand; three, one-thousand; four, one-thousand. And exhale. One, one-thousand; two, one-thousand; three, one-thousand; four, one-thousand."

Follow up by saying something like "You are sitting in your living room, in that comfy arm chair that you keep by the window". This "present time" statement after the breathing exercise provides a baseline for directing the person in distress further into present time, reduces anxiety, and helps her regain a normal breathing pattern. Once this is accomplished, you can begin discussing the reason she called. If you attempt to discuss her crisis without first getting the caller into present time, it will be difficult to discern if the caller is really able to hear what you are saying.

Callers to emergency lines are often anxious and, as a result, their breathing is labored. A dispatcher can hear a person's internal struggle as a caller inhales with a wheeze. Emergency dispatchers nevertheless need to get information. If the caller is completely unable to speak due to his failed attempts to breathe, the dispatcher may ask the person to take a slow breath in and exhale, and then ask him for the information again. "Sir. Take a big breath in and exhale slowly. Good. Now what is the name of the street where you saw the car accident?"

Stress Relaxation Exercise

While working in a residential setting, I enjoyed facilitating a breathing activity for clients. Staff who came on the next shift would invariably comment on how quiet and relaxed the group was. Clients, I noticed, welcomed the opportunity to learn to relax.

You can practice the following stress relaxation exercise yourself, or you can facilitate this calming technique for others. The goal of the exercise is to guide the body toward relaxation and breathing that is slow, deep, and deliberate.

Suffice to say, I have guided many different groups of people through this exercise, and it is not unusual for some to actually fall asleep while participating. Don't be surprised if you hear someone in the room breathing loudly or even snoring. Consider it as the sign of a job well done.

To begin, find your baseline heart rate. Check your pulse by placing your fingertips on the carotid artery, right below the joint connecting the jaw to the skull. Open and close your mouth to find the hinge and then move your fingers downward toward your throat until you feel the pulse. Time your pulse for ten seconds and multiply by six.

13 x 6 = 78 beats per minute.

Setting the Pace – Stress Relaxation Exercise

Begin the exercise by inhaling slowly to a count of four. Think to yourself or have someone else say out loud:

One, one-thousand; two, one-thousand; three, one-thousand; four, one-thousand.

Think about filling your stomach area or lower lungs first. Hold your breath in for a three second count:

One, one-thousand; two, one-thousand; three, one-thousand.

Exhale slowly to a count of four.

One, one-thousand; two, one-thousand; three, one-thousand; four, one-thousand.

Do this three times, then increase to a five count, hold for a four count, and exhale to a five count. After ten cycles, check your pulse at the carotid artery again. When done correctly, such an exercise can dramatically reduce your respiration and heart rate. At first you may not notice a drop in your pulse rate. If this is a new concept, it may take time to teach the body to relax. You can try doing more than ten cycles. Remember that you might want to increase the count as you go along, which helps to further slow your breathing. Slow, deep breaths ensure that the brain is receiving plenty of oxygen.

Breathing exercises are great for reducing the anxiety associated with fear or uncertainty. With practice, you can use this stress relaxation exercise before, during, and after an intervention.

I like to begin and end each Aikido class with a breathing exercise. Each of us leads very busy lives, and after a full day, it feels right to sit quietly at the beginning of class and reflect on the simple act of breathing. During class, I constantly remind students to breathe, especially when I notice that their bodies look stiff or their faces look tightly held, grimacing. As students breathe, their shoulders drop and their faces relax. At the end of every class, we purposely focus our breathing once more to slow ourselves down after an active workout.

We have had weekly children's classes for students between seven and twelve years of age led by Sensei Charles Gilliam since 2000. Years ago Charles' son, Gabe, and another long time student's son, Nico, would each have to wait in the gym for the adult's class to finish. The two boys would run around the gym, playing games and doing what children do—play loudly. The room, as you might imagine, would be filled with giggles and flying Frisbees. Often it became downright loud, and sometimes we'd have to ask the children to lower their voices. Fellow Aikido practicing readers are probably surprised to hear that we allowed the children to play loudly and be so disruptive. I see practicing in a noisy room as a good lesson for the adults in the practice of staying focused, as one would need to do in an actual, real life intervention. Rarely is an attack or intervention quiet. Being able to keep your focus in a setting that is noisy and disruptive, though not necessary for every class, is, on occasion, well worth the experience. The two boys also gained more than just playtime. At the end of the adult class, while we were doing our closing breath exercise, the children would hush each other and grow silent. It was as if their bodies were swept along by the power of purposeful breathing, as if everyone in the room shared the same, concerted breath.

The Power of Suggestion

Medical personnel administer oxygen when a person is having difficulty breathing in order to sustain the organs and brain. Most other crisis interveners don't have a supply of oxygen available, but we all can supply the power of suggestion. (Please note that while breathing-relaxation techniques can be used in conjunction with oxygen and emergency medical resuscitation when a person is in physical distress, they cannot replace medical intervention techniques.) As an EMT, the visible relief of patients in trauma often amazed me when I suggested, "Think about your breathing." I could almost read their thoughts as the expression on their faces changed from grimace to one that indicated, "Oh, yeah, I can do that." When a person is frightened, whether because of a medical or emotional emergency, encouraging her to focus on her breathing is a tangible act and a wonderfully grounding task. When confronted by pain, fear, or an overwhelming obstacle, it is comforting to know that we can still control our breath.

Suggesting slower breaths or providing a count: "Breathe in: one, two, three, four. Hold it: one, two, and three. Breathe out:

one, two, three, four," has an immediate impact on a person's well-being. Inadequate ventilation makes people feel dizzy, listless, and frightened. As soon as the level of oxygen is increased, the body is able to relax and a renewed sense of well-being results. The following example illustrates this.

Breathing with a Patient

The station wagon had rolled over the guardrail on the side of the highway. Everyone was still in the car except for the driver, who had been thrown about twenty-five yards away against a cyclone fence. She had not been wearing a seat belt.

She lay face down, motionless. An off-duty state trooper had dug out the soil around her face so she could breathe. Without any medical supplies except for my woolen blanket for shock, and therefore, seemingly unable to help her, he and I felt desperate. She had a weak pulse and shallow breathing. I kept asking her to stay with us and listen to her breathing. Coaxing, I repeated, "Breathe easy. That's good," over and over. With the sirens wailing in the distance, she started to moan. She began to move as if reaching up. I had already surmised that she was the mother of the two kids still in the car. I said, "The girls are safe. They still need you." And then her body relaxed. The three of us were breathing in unison as the stretcher was brought down the embankment.

This woman had been expending all her energy moaning and trying to move. Reducing her anxiety and giving her direction in the form of a focus on breathing helped her relax and provided her brain with critically needed oxygen. At the same time, I reminded the woman that her daughters were dependent upon her. I didn't want her to relax so completely that she might give up the fight for her life. (Remember that setting a rhythm to follow, such as a count, or repeating "Breathe" should follow the initial suggestion to breathe.)

If a Technique Works, Pass It On

I never hide my strategy for de-escalating a crisis. People don't like feeling that they are being manipulated and will say so. "I know what you are doing. You can't make me stop if I don't want to!" Instead of being offended by an obstinate reply, I consider it useful information—at least they heard me. They may not understand the entire motive behind my actions, but at least I am not being ignored. My reply could be, "Thanks, I respect you and appreciate your awareness," a statement that usually provides a pause, since angry people never expect to be thanked. I could also say, "It's good that you see what I am doing. I need your attention and help to work this out." People in distress need calm, skilled guidance to gain self-control. In time, they may use the same techniques with another client, friend, or family member.

Breathe Sign

When a colleague of mine was visiting from out-of-state, I gave her driving directions and put up a sign on the telephone pole near my house that I knew she couldn't miss. On an old piece of wood with a green magic marker, I wrote the word Breathe.

At the time, I lived on the Wendell Town Common, a classic New England setting with century-old, white meeting halls, a one-room library, a bandstand, and surrounding homes. She told me with a laugh as she got out of her car that she knew I was close by when she saw the sign. My friend knew about my association with breathing as a conflict management technique.

I left the sign up, and it was there for over a year. From time to time, I would overhear townspeople talk about the sign. "You know, each time I drive by that 'Breathe' sign, I just take in a deep breath. It's a good reminder."

In 1995, the *Boston Globe Magazine* had a feature article called "A Town Like Wendell." To my surprise, in the center of the article was a small paragraph stating, "On the edge of the common, tacked to a pole at the corner of Locke's Hill and Center Road, is a hand-painted sign that reads, simply, "Breathe.'"

In Summary

The impact of the unplanned experiment of the 'Breathe' sign deepened my conviction about the value of simple and practical interventions. Redirecting conflict means using tools that will empower those in crisis to regain self-control. Whether intervening during a conflict or a medical emergency, the influence of breath has never failed to impress me. For the intervener, in the heat of the moment, remembering to breathe or helping others breathe is no small task. Exhaling is the first essential step toward maintaining a normal rate of respiration. Then, the intervener can guide others in normalizing their breathing as a means of restoring self-control. Breathing awareness is a powerful tool for effective intervention and yet another way of creating a safe scene.

Cause No Harm

The Way of a Warrior is based on humanity, love, and sincerity; the heart of martial valor is true bravery, wisdom, love, and friendship. Emphasis on the physical aspects of warriorship is futile, for the power of the body is always limited.

— Morihei Ueshiba, founder of Aikido

When asked how Aikido differs from other martial arts, I prefer to bow out of trying to make comparisons. I truly only know about Aikido, and even after years of practice with this martial art, I still feel like a beginner. Aikido, like any art form, develops an ever-growing depth of both knowledge and wisdom through practice.

The allure of Aikido and why I have continued in my practice is another matter and one that I do enjoy expounding upon. The physical movements of Aikido are beneficial for one's body, beautiful to watch, and a joy to experience. You learn to equally employ both the right side and left side of your body. Over years of practice, Aikidoists build a sense of ambidexterity not only with their hands, but also with their whole body. Learning to move with an inner sense of calm and balance is a very special reward that continual practice provides. Beyond the physical elements of Aikido is the philosophy. At its best, it can be summed up as: Cause no harm.

There are people who, if left to their own devices, would hurt others or themselves. Aikido provides the resources for safely and humanely helping a person who is a danger. I wish that there were never a need to physically restrain a person, and though that day seems closer to me now more than ever, at least for mental health workers, by and large for the rest of society, containment is still an unfortunate but necessary measure. Therefore, I constantly seek to review how to help people who are dangerous to themselves or others—and to do so with the specific intention of causing no harm.

One of my roles as a consultant in the field of conflict management is to review use of force policies or what is called by psychiatric hospitals "the use of restraint and seclusion." When you see the phrase use of force, it may conjure up images of men in white putting a straitjacket on a person. Perhaps it rekindles memories of the 1991 incident involving a group of Los Angles police officers caught in the act of brutally beating Rodney King Jr., after he was pulled over for a traffic violation. More recently we can look to political riffs in the world, such as Iran's 2009 crack-down on political protesters. "Yuck," you may be thinking, "I don't want to read about manhandling a person." Or you might still be scratching your head trying to figure out what exactly is the use of force.

Use of Force Defined

Use of force as defined in the context of conflict management is the use of a hands-on technique. A hands-on technique consists of any and all physical contact, such as holding a person's wrist or placing a hand on another person's arm in order to guide and escort. For the human service community of workers and educators, there should not be any need for brute force when applying hands-on. Since the term "use of force" implies an element of coercion, I will use the term "hands-on" in this chapter to distinguish it from the use of force. The distinction is necessary, since the Response Crisis Intervention Model teaches hands-on techniques that allow freedom of movement, i.e. the person in crisis can lift his arms, legs, and feet, if he so desires. Instead of the need for oppositional force by the intervener, practitioners of the Response Crisis Intervention Model avoid the use of brute force or any force at all, for that matter, when applying a hands-on technique. You will also note that I do not use the term restraint, but instead call all physical interventions "hands-on." Restraint implies controlling or limiting movement. Though there is a degree of limitation when a person is being held and hands-on is applied, I prefer to encourage practitioners of the Response Crisis Intervention Model to use the term escort, versus restraint. It is a subtle difference, and yet one worthy to note. If an intervener goes in with the mindset of escorting a person, they are more likely to avoid the use of brute force; whereas, if an intervener goes in with the mindset of applying a restraint, intrinsic to this term is the limitation of movement.

The sectors of our society that use some form of hands-on are wide-ranging and diverse. The following are just a few: the military, law enforcement, education, residential treatment settings, parents and guardians, and hospitals. There is a great difference between the use of hands-on in law enforcement and hands-on in educational settings. Despite the different types of hands-on techniques used at one site versus another, there is a general standard denoting when a hands-on technique is authorized.

This chapter will explore the use of hands-on as a conflict management tool and the need for a universal code of conduct for this type of intervention. For workers who are expected to use hands-on as part of their job duties, this chapter will be especially helpful. Although hands-on is a fairly clinical term, think twice before skipping over this chapter. Everyone, whether parent or professional intervener, family member or patient, is impacted by the use of hands-on interventions in our society.

Deadly Force

I have found that most people would prefer to either completely ignore the topic of hands-on or talk about the use of hands-on behind closed doors. The risk of injury for all parties involved in the application of hands-on contributes to reluctance about discussing it. *The Hartford Courant's* five-part series in 1998 called "Deadly Restraint" sent a shiver of concern for human service providers across the nation. It also led to the passage of legislation that required hospitals to report deaths caused by restraints or risk losing Medicaid funding. The series began with the heading, "Hundreds of the nation's most vulnerable have been killed by the system intended to care for them." One particular restraint technique, crossing a person's arms across his or her chest and pinning him or her in this position face down upon the floor, was found to be a potentially deadly hold, particularly for children. *The Hartford Courant's* findings from a fifty state survey "confirmed 142 deaths during or shortly after restraint or seclusion in the past decade."

The discussion on the need to use hands-on and what is deemed as a reasonable amount of force continues to evolve. Restraint and seclusion policies can appear vague from the outset. There are so many "what ifs" involved in real life conflicts, such as, "What if my facility says that I can't use hands-on, but I walk into a room and find a person being beaten up? What do I do then? Do I just call the police and watch that person being killed?" or "If I see a child in my classroom about to attack another student with a sharp pencil, can I intervene?"

To both queries the answer is to use common sense. Many work sites do not authorize employees to use hands-on. Such sites cannot justify having a worker like a teacher leave a group of students unsupervised while he or she tries to break up a fight between two people. To do so would put not only the teacher, but also the rest of the students at risk of harm. Challenges to rules governing the use of hands-on, such as the teacher who stops a student from stabbing another child with a pencil will continue. Despite the fact that reaching for the student's hand to prevent the stabbing appears to be an obvious course of action, the teacher may nevertheless be asked to file a report or, worse, face a lawsuit. We live in very litigious times. Even when you are authorized to use hands-on, you may still be investigated to determine if you truly exhausted all your resources before choosing to intervene physically.

Hands-on Complicates Conflict Management

The intervener's goal is: to cause no harm. Your intention, then, when entering a scene that has escalated to the point where physical management is necessary, will govern the techniques you choose. A person whose only recourse is to meet violence with greater violence will indeed complicate matters by using excessive force. If you are the intervener who must use hands-on, maintain self-control and keep your goals in order.

When Is the Use of Hands-on Permissible?

The most widely-used standard permitting the use of hands-on during conflict management is stated as follows: It is permissible to use hands-on when a person is a danger to self or others.

Attempting to commit suicide is an example of endangering one's own life. A police officer who reaches for a person trying to jump from a bridge exemplifies a permissible use of hands-on.

School administrators and teachers are the guardians of the student body. A student may be considered at risk if she leaves a classroom or exits the building without supervision. The following vignette examines authorized use of hands-on in a classroom setting.

A Student at Risk

> *Mr. Stine had noticed that Billy was not working on his assignment with the rest of the third graders in his special needs' classroom. Mr. Stine had wanted to go over and help Billy out, but the teacher's assistant had called in sick that morning, and Mr. Stine was overwhelmed. "I'll be with you in a minute, Billy, to help you out, okay?" called out*

Mr. Stine to the daydreaming boy across the room. When Billy didn't acknowledge him, Mr. Stine knew that the boy's behavior would only get worse. When he looked up again, Billy had moved to the door and was starting to leave the room.

"Billy, wait a minute," Mr. Stine called. But Billy was already out the door and into the hallway.

Behavior of this type happens every day at schools across the land. For the most part, educators are able to reason with a student who leaves a classroom or a school building. Talking is and should always be the first choice, but a third grader's safety is considered at risk when he leaves a classroom or school building without permission. Depending upon staffing availability, training, and the school district's policy on authorized use of hands-on and protocol, Mr. Stine could very well be within his rights as a teacher to stop Billy physically.

Can Billy be Physically Stopped in a Safe Manner?

Grabbing Billy by the wrist as his mother might do when leading him across a busy intersection is not considered to be a safe physical hold. Crisis intervention training programs that specialize in physical management techniques teach hands-on techniques that are designed to minimize the risk of injury to both the person being escorted and the intervener. Protecting interveners from jabbing elbows and keeping a person's limbs close to his or her sides decreases the likelihood of injury for all parties involved during a hands-on intervention.

Although leading Billy by the wrist may work, it is not considered a safe intervention because his elbow is not secured from swinging out and hitting the intervener. In addition, Billy's arm and shoulder are at risk of being pulled in a way that could cause harm for the youngster.

If you have read this far, I must have your attention, but you may still be thinking, "Holy smokes. If I were Billy's parent, I would just grab his wrist." Perhaps you would, especially if that type of grab is all you know. Parents do have more leeway in using force on their own children. I believe, though, that parents and guardians are actively seeking disciplinary options that, in the end, cause no mental or physical harm to their child. If there are other options available, you can be sure that parents and instructors of crisis intervention trainings will seek out the least injurious technique for all parties.

Other Options besides using Hands-on to Manage Billy

There is always an opportunity to exercise less invasive interventions. An alternative to using hands-on in this student's case is to assign a staff member to follow Billy from a distance. Meanwhile, a parent / guardian and the police should be notified if he leaves the building. Educators have often discussed such scenarios during my seminars and all agree that a student will typically act as if she is leaving the grounds, but will instead hide behind a swing set or a tree while she cools down her temper. Once done, she will return to the classroom and willingly participate.

The Goal of a Hands-on Intervention

Although the use of hands-on may be authorized in Billy's case, there are alternatives to exercising its use. Notifying parents and watching Billy from a distance does take time away from educators who are already overburdened with responsibilities. Yet, with or without the use of hands-on, this intervention is going to take time. If Billy is physically stopped from leaving school grounds, he is likely to become combative and will need a supervised cooling-down time.

Billy and the interveners are equally at risk if the decision is to use "hands-on." Bumps and bruises can be expected even when state-of-the-art physical management techniques are used. And what about the other students, teachers, or visitors who will witness the use of hands-on? Bearing witness to a physical intervention is not a pleasant experience. In fact, it can have a terrorizing impact that is long-lasting. Not only will Billy need to be attended to once the initial intervention is over, but all who witness the intervention should be debriefed and assessed to make sure that they feel safe and not fearful of being harmed themselves.

Mr. Stine had felt that the scene was likely to escalate, but he was working solo, and this complicated matters. Leaving one student to attend to another may not only have failed to keep Billy in the classroom, but it may have caused a chain reaction of events: "What about me, Mr. Stine?"

"Billy gets all the attention." "I thought you were going to help me!"

When you are responsible for a group of people, you have to weigh in how your choice will impact not only the individual, but also the entire group.

A Student at Risk – Take 2

Mr. Stine decided to call the vice-principal's office and inform the secretary of Billy's departure. She, in turn, notified the vice-principal who then walked up the hallway and met Billy walking toward the main office. Billy did not reply to the vice-principal's greeting but did, however, walk with the vice-principal to the main office. Once in the office, Billy took a seat. The vice-principal kept a watchful eye on the boy and, after five minutes of sitting, Billy was able to move into the vice-principal's office and discuss his behavior in Mr. Stine's class.

A hands-on intervention was avoided in Billy's case because he did not run from the vice-principal's care and was able to regain a sense of self-control, demonstrated by his willingness to sit quietly in the main office.

The Unskilled Use of Force and a Feeling of Hopelessness

The fight-or-flight response to conflict can prompt you to flee a scene, respond verbally, or engage in hand-to-hand combat in an attempt to control an incident. The ability to manage a conflict effectively is virtually nil if one's self-control is compromised. Feelings of hopelessness, fear of injury, and fear of loss of self-control all ignite an emotional response. An emotional response with an unskilled use of a hands-on technique increases the likelihood of inflicting harm. Interveners may then resort to street fighting maneuvers, military combat moves, or frantic flailing at anyone who comes into their grasp.

There are many dangerous "techniques" used by unskilled interveners: choke holds, strikes and kicks to the head or abdomen, bear hugs that compromise another's oxygen supply, and shoving, slapping, and poking that deliver substantial, if not life threatening, injuries.

A Father's Misuse of Force

> *Nick Carson heard banging on the ceiling above his head and knew that his two teenage boys were probably fighting again. They had been at each other's throats all day, and Nick was tired of it all. He walked upstairs and opened their bedroom door. Nick walked into the boy's room without a pause and hit the boy closer to him on the side of head with a strong, right-handed slap. Alex dropped to the floor like a dead weight and didn't get up. "You want some too, Benny?" shouted Nick. Benny had backed off instantly when he saw his father slap Alex. "Get up, Alex. I want this room cleaned up. It looks like a pig sty." Alex was laid out on the floor. His teeth were clenched and his body was rigid.*
>
> *When Nick saw the appearance of Alex's face, he knew instantly there was something wrong with his son. "Oh, no, what have I done?" cried the father.*

Physical force should not be used as a punitive measure during conflict management. Addressing consequences is part of the crisis-conflict resolution stage. This is not to say that the father should slap his son on the side of the head once he has secured scene safety. Nick should not slap Alex or Benny on the side of the head in anger or at all. Assaultive behavior is never productive and typically causes serious physical and mental harm to the recipient.

Nick didn't even try to distract his sons or command them to stop fighting. If a family's level of communication is so stressed that two sons ignore their own father's demands, the police should be called. Taking matters into one's own hands under such circumstances will only serve to further escalate the conflict. Perhaps, on occasion, Nick would be physically able to stop his sons from fighting. How many times can a parent intercede in this manner without also putting herself at risk and causing physical harm to her child? Addressing consequences when you are in control of your emotions and not acting with blind rage is a sound practice and protects everyone involved from undue harm.

Let's give Nick another chance to manage his son's fight. This time, he won't use force.

A Father's Misuse of Force – Take 2

Nick heard banging on the ceiling above his head and knew that his two teenage boys were probably fighting again. They had been at each other's throats all day, and Nick was tired of it all. He walked upstairs and opened their bedroom door and stood for a moment. Alex had his arm wrapped around Benny's head. "Say you're sorry or I won't let go." Benny was bent over and squealing, "No way."

In a loud and steady voice, their father said, "Alex. Let Benny go." Nick then took two steps forward into the boys' room. Alex reluctantly shoved Benny away from him. "Benny, go downstairs and wait for me in the living room, son." Benny left the room without looking back.

With the two boys separated, the target of their immediate anger has been removed. The father is now in a better position to mediate the dispute with each boy separately. Initially pausing at the door and taking his time to assess the scene not only gave Nick Carson time to compose himself, but it also made his intervention stand out. If he had entered the room without stopping and demanded that Alex let go of his brother, Alex may not have immediately noticed him. Quiet composure in the midst of chaos is an effective technique that catches the attention of those in conflict.

Hands-off Policies and their Effect on Workers

Workers who must follow the hands-off policy of their work site often feel frustrated or helpless. "Are we expected to just stand there and watch as another person is being beaten up? I just couldn't do that. I would have to try to stop the fight!" said Mark, a direct care staff member at an emergency shelter for juveniles. For Mark, compromising his compassion goes against the very reason he entered the human service field. Yet, injuries are likely when you fail to follow a work site protocol. If there is an inadequate staff-to-client ratio, one staff person intervening puts the rest of his charges at risk if the worker is injured.

Work sites that have a hands-off policy, meaning that employees are not to use hands-on when intervening, rely instead on the local police to assist. Relinquishing authority to the police can create conflicts for the requesting agency, however. Once the police are involved, it is the police who have jurisdiction over the scene, possibly compounding the workers' initial feelings of hopelessness in having had to make the call.

Professionals who work at sites that serve aggressive people should be provided with ongoing training in verbal intervention. Policies and procedures regarding the management of aggressive behavior should be reviewed with employees to ensure that appropriate emergency protocols will be followed if a violent scene erupts.

Job Descriptions in Relation to Hands-on

For work sites that do authorize use of hands-on interventions, clarification is essential as to when and to what degree an employee is expected to intervene physically. In facilities serving a potentially aggressive population, job descriptions will often include statements like the following:

- "Workers may be required to use physical restraints."

This statement gets right to the point. Other descriptions are not as straightforward.

- "Workers are responsible for the security and well-being of the [clients, students, patients]."

Clarification on the particulars of one's job duties as they pertain to hands-on interventions should be found in the agency's policies and procedures manual.

Policies and Procedures Regarding Hands-on

How far do you go in assuring the welfare of another person? If one client is being assaulted by another, should the police be called or should workers physically intervene? Organizations that authorize the use of hands-on should have a policy that describes when hands-on can and cannot be used.

A hands-on policy might include the following clauses that clearly define when the welfare of a person is at risk and when hands-on can be used.

Authorized use of hands-on can be invoked only when:

- A person is a danger to self or others
- A person will not follow a directive

Some policies will also authorize workers to use hands-on in the following situations:

- Self defense

- To prevent people from inflicting major property damage

Along with the job description, the hands-on policy tells workers what their duties are in terms of "providing for the safety and well-being of the [clients, students, patients]" by more clearly defining the following

- Doctor's authorization is necessary for use of hands-on
- Amount of time restraint can be applied
- Medical follow-up should always be sought afterwards

The policy governing the use of hands-on should clearly state which techniques are authorized to be used by workers.

For example:

Workers can only use the techniques that are specifically taught during the on-site crisis intervention training.

Hands-on Abuse in the Classroom Setting

Gary and Martha worked as teacher assistants at an elementary school. They were both trained crisis interveners and were the first ones called when a child became disruptive.

Peter, an eleven-year-old student, refused to participate in the lesson being taught by his teacher. He pushed over his chair, and the other children backed away. His teacher called the main office. The secretary, in turn, called Gary and Martha, who were both temporarily relieved of their duties. When Gary and Martha asked Peter to come with them into the hallway, Peter kicked at Gary and hit him directly in the shin.

When Martha asked Gary if he was okay, Gary said, "Just fine. Let's go!" while moving toward Peter. Gary put his hands on Peter, and Martha followed her coworker. While Peter was being held, he was yelling, "You're hurting me! Let go!"

Martha saw that Gary's knuckles were turning white while he gripped Peter's wrist. "Loosen up, Gary," said Martha. Gary ignored his coworker and held on tighter. "Gary!" demanded Martha, "Loosen up now!"

Gary was unable to control his impulse of wanting to get even with Peter for kicking him. His tightening grip, white knuckles, and unwillingness to listen to Martha indicated that Gary was unable to control his emotions.

Interventions like Gary's demonstrate the need for maintaining professionalism and self-control. Getting kicked or spit at are some of the indignities that an employee can experience in work environments that serve potentially volatile people. Learning how to control the impulse to react during an intervention should be part of every crisis intervention training.

Sometimes, despite impulse control, the best option is to leave the intervention and let another worker who is not emotionally tied to the incident take over. When Gary was kicked, he should have backed away from the scene and composed himself. If he could not let go of his anger toward Peter for kicking him in the shin, Gary should have excused himself and had someone else, such as the principal, step in and take over his role as intervener. When a worker has become emotionally reactive, he should leave the scene. A common code used by coworkers to give space to another is, "You have a phone call," a euphemistic way of saying take a time-out.

Using "You got a phone Call" Exit Strategy

As explained earlier in Chapter Three, The Response Crisis Intervention Model uses a two-tiered code for checking in on a co-worker. Level One is to determine if the intervener needs assistance by stating, "You have a phone call." If the intervention is progressing well, and the intervener does not want to exit, he can decline the phone call by responding, "Tell them I will call back." The Level Two statement, "The doctor is on the phone," is used when co-workers have determined that the intervener is too emotionally caught up in the intervention. As a protocol, the Level Two phone intercept means: Step out of the intervention.

Martha could have tried to help Gary right after he got hit by saying, "Hold up. Let's both take a deep breath with Peter and try this over again." Such a statement also takes into account the person in crisis and would reset the mood for an intervention that has started off on the wrong foot. Another option might have been to move Peter's classmates to another room, a viable option used by many schools. With the removal of spectators, an angry person will be better able to focus on the situation at hand without feeling the need to perform in front of peers.

Authorization and Amount of Time Hands-on Can Be Used

The policy governing use of hands-on should contain a statement describing who can authorize a physical intervention—usually a supervisor or doctor. The length of time that hands-on can be used should also be part of every policy. For instance, the policy might state that a person can be held for up to five minutes, at which time a doctor or supervisor has to provide authorization for hands-on to continue. Without such guidelines, a person could theoretically be held indefinitely.

Assessing a person's readiness to be released from a hands-on technique is a procedure that should be taught to workers during crisis intervention training. Regaining a normal breathing pattern, verbally acknowledging those who are intervening, and agreeing to the parameters of the release are three indicators used to determine a person's readiness to be released.

Medical Follow-Up

Providing medical follow-up after a restraint promotes quality of care for both the person who was held and the intervener. At times, people do get injured during physical interventions. Medical review helps to determine if the application of a hands-on technique was done properly or if the physical hold being applied is contributing to a particular injury. *The Hartford Courant's* series brought to light a particular hold that was responsible for a number of deaths throughout the United States. The facedown floor hold, with a person's arms held under his or her own body, has since been banned. Unfortunately, it took a journalistic exposé to discredit a long-used restraint that might have been banned far sooner through appropriate in-house reviews.

When a person has been physically held, a medical examination should be done afterwards. Using the local hospital or having a nurse on call is an option for agencies that wish to incorporate a medical follow-up into their hands-on policy. Employees should be taught how to document an incident, and they should understand who reviews the form, and how.

Gray Areas in the Use of Hands-on

The following examples illustrate some of the most common queries into hands-on policies. For professional interveners, it is advisable to review questions during in-service trainings in order to clarify misconceptions on the use of hands-on.

Destruction of Property–The Broken Pencil

Nancy Shelborn was a teacher at a residential treatment center for adolescents. Her agency's hands-on policy specified that staff had the right to use hands-on if one of the following existed:

- *the student was in danger of harming herself or others*
- *the student did not follow a directive*
- *the student was destroying property*

During Ms. Shelborn's Wednesday morning class with a group of girls, she noticed that Tracy Adams was whispering to another girl and pointing at Patty Fisch. Ms. Shelborn said, "Tracy, is there something going on that you would like to share with the rest of us?"

Tracy replied, "That bitch there has my shirt, and staff let her get away with it. She's got to pay her dues."

Ms. Shelborn stepped up to Tracy's desk and said, "You get one consequence for swearing. For threatening another student—"

Tracy cut her off: "Yeah, and what do I get for breaking this pencil? A trip to Disney World?" The rest of the class exploded with laughter when Tracy defiantly broke the pencil in half.

Had Ms. Shelborn found herself in a situation that justified the use of hands-on? Although the policy said she had the right to use hands-on if there were destruction of property, did breaking a pencil merit the use of hands-on? Had Ms. Shelborn fully exhausted her verbal skills? Was this destruction of property a threat to others or Tracy? All of these questions can come to mind whenever an intervener is confronted with a situation that is potentially volatile.

She could certainly make a convincing argument for needing to use hands-on by stating that the student was inciting the class and was therefore a danger to herself and others. Resorting to hands-on, though, should only be done after an intervener has exhausted all possible alternatives for managing a scene. Conflict management does not consist solely of knowing what to say to a person; it also requires an understanding of how you portray and project your position of authority. Let's review how Ms. Shelborn provoked a potentially manageable situation into a conflict.

Ms. Shelborn's first intervention pushed Tracy into a position in which she had to respond in a fashion so as not to "lose face" in front of her peers. Tracy was doing the right thing by telling the teacher exactly why she was upset. She could have lied and said, "Nothing," or she could have made up a story, such as, "Oh, we were just talking about the movie last night." Instead of forming an alliance with the student based upon her truthfulness, Ms. Shelborn boxed Tracy into a position where she had nothing left to lose by being defiant. The incident was blown out of proportion and perhaps even taught the student to lie next time instead of telling the truth.

The situation started as a manageable conflict, but through her own error, the teacher escalated the incident into a standoff between herself and the student. Ms. Shelborn should continue to intervene verbally and avoid physical intervention at all costs. Breaking a pencil can indeed become a physical threat, in the same way that any implement held in one's hand can potentially be used as a weapon. Ms. Shelborn should have determined if this pencil was going to be a weapon or simply a theatrical prop used by the student.

Using the same scenario, let's give Ms. Shelborn another chance at working with Tracy.

Destruction of Property – The Broken Pencil – Take 2

> *During Nancy Shelborn's Wednesday morning class with a group of girls, she noticed that Tracy Adams was whispering to another girl and pointing at Patty Fisch. Ms. Shelborn said, "Tracy, is there something going on that you would like to share with the rest of us?"*
>
> *Tracy replied, "That bitch there has my shirt, and staff let her get away with it. She's got to pay her dues."*
>
> *Ms. Shelborn stepped up to Tracy's desk and said, "Thanks for telling me that. You do have a lot going on."*
>
> *The teacher then turned slightly to face the rest of the class. She knew that the other students had overheard this brief exchange. Patty, meanwhile, was looking forward at the blackboard in a stoic pose.*

"All right, everyone," the teacher began. "Now I'm going to give Tracy some advice that you are welcome to listen to. I do not, however, expect any outbursts."

Ms. Shelborn turned back to Tracy and said, "You are on the right track by speaking about a conflict. I am recommending that you continue to speak to a staff member back at your cottage, or you can stay to speak with me after class."

"Yeah, whatever," Tracy replied.

"Whatever is not how I see it. It's all about caring and making the right choices," said the teacher. Ms. Shelborn then walked over to Patty's desk and encouraged her also to stay after class.

Ms. Shelborn used the situation as a teaching moment in both of the preceding examples. She also set a boundary by telling the students what was acceptable behavior: no outbursts. This time, hands-on never became an issue. Working with Tracy is less time consuming than managing a scene that requires a use of hands-on. Both the teacher and the students benefit from such interventions.

Major Property Damage–Erik's Fluorescent Bulb

The psychiatric hospital for men and women was an older building, and the state was in the process of securing money to build a new state-of-the-art facility. But in its current condition, tiles were missing from the floors and the overhead lighting was less than adequate. Employees were constantly on alert for patients getting their hands on loose debris from the already dilapidated building.

Cheryl and John, who worked second shift, were both in the staff office finishing up paperwork. The other three workers were in the social room talking and playing cards with patients. It was seven o'clock in the evening, and everyone gathered as usual in the social room to wind down after a long day.

The restraint policy at the hospital stated that staff members were authorized to use hands-on to prevent patients from harming themselves or others.

Cheryl and John were first on the scene after they heard Erik, a patient, yelling out from the library. They found Erik standing in the middle of the reading room holding a four-foot long fluorescent bulb and shouting out, "All right, men. The enemy is in our sight!" Erik then kicked over a large oak table in the center of the room and hid behind it. Cheryl immediately called for additional assistance, and soon there were six hospital workers on the scene. John was talking to Erik from the hallway. Erik responded by shouting out, "Fire!" and throwing a ball of paper he had torn from a book.

The staffing team on hand decided to wait out Erik's behavior until he initiated a "peace treaty." The fluorescent bulb in Erik's hand presented too great a risk of danger for Erik and the staff, since toxic dust and glass fragments would be released if he broke the bulb. Meanwhile, one team member called the police to help assist if Erik did, indeed, decide to break the bulb. Erik appeared to be content behind his barricade in the library, since he was making no move to leave the room. The supervisor on duty hoped to avoid the risk of wrestling away a large fluorescent bulb from a psychotic patient.

Erik did break the bulb in half and started toward the door leading out of the library. The police arrived at the same time and stood at the entrance to the library. When Erik saw the two police officers in uniform, he immediately put down his weapon and walked compliantly out of the room.

Even when there is authorization to use hands-on, it may still be in everyone's best interest to bring in police assistance. Intervening when a person is holding a knife or, in this case, a long glass lighting fixture that contains toxic chemicals requires sophisticated skills in physical intervention.

The police have a number of options available to them. Their decision to physically intervene will be based upon whether they are being directly targeted, whether the person is targeting someone else, or whether the person is trying to inflict injury upon himself.

On-site security or police officers are often called to hospital emergency rooms to stand by in case a patient becomes disruptive. I have worked with officers who have moved in too quickly, thereby escalating a scene that might have been managed verbally. For instance, while working in an ER with a young man who had attempted suicide, it was my role to tell him that he was being involuntarily admitted to a psychiatric hospital for further evaluation. I had met with the police officers when they first arrived. They were called in to act as back up in case the patient became volatile while I told him about the commitment proceedings. I had asked them to stand by while I spoke to the patient, but they made their presence known as soon as I approached the young man. Although the patient was not being combative as I spoke to him, he became loud and disrespectful toward us as the officers on duty moved toward him.

Relinquishing control of a scene to the police decreases the likelihood of harm to staff and patients. However to do so, means that the police officers are now in command of the scene, which is not always a good option for mental health workers and their patients. Maintaining an active dialogue with the local police department is a proactive measure for any facility that works with a volatile population, even if there is a hands-on policy allowing staff to physically intervene.

Avoiding Physical Intervention – Bus Number 7

Everything was going smoothly on Wednesday morning as the buses were arriving at the middle school. Then Bus Number 7 pulled into the school grounds. Jack Cann, the vice-principal, and Lee Wu, the teacher on duty that morning, immediately noticed Bus Number 7 as it moved up to the front of the building. All the children on the bus looked as if they were standing. When the bus door opened, Mr. Cann stepped up to the door and looked to Frances Holmes, the driver, for an explanation. She immediately said, "Sam is yelling at another boy in the back of the bus. I think he is starting a fight."

If Sam and the other boy begin fighting, should Mr. Cann immediately intervene and break up the fight?

Mr. Cann knew that safety was the first priority. His personal safety was not at risk. The scene on the bus, though, was definitely not safe, and he was responsible for the entire busload of children. The quickest way to make the majority of the children safe was to get them off the bus. Mr. Cann instructed Mr. Wu and Mrs. Holmes to quickly and quietly assist the rest of the students off the bus. He then began to move to the back of the bus. Sam was yelling at another boy who was cornered in the farthest seat in the back. The other boy looked pleadingly at Mr. Cann.

Mr. Cann said, "Sam, it is time to get off the bus."

Sam replied, "I'm not leaving until he gives me my money." The bus had emptied, and Mr. Cann saw that Mr. Wu was standing outside the back door of the bus to provide assistance if necessary.

If Mr. Cann tried to forcefully move Sam off the bus, the risk of injury would be high in such closed quarters. In general, it is always best to allow an agitated person to move of his or her own accord. Mr. Cann decided that since Sam was acknowledging him, there was a chance for further dialogue.

The vice-principal sat in the seat in front of Sam and the other boy. "I want to help out, Sam," he said, "but this bus has to move out to pick up the kids going to the high school. How about stepping off the bus so you can tell me what's up?"

"I don't want to leave until he pays me back," said Sam.

"I hear that, but this bus has got to keep moving and we all have to get off," Mr. Cann said softly.

"Get another bus," yelled Sam.

"Sam, I'm here to help you," said Mr. Cann.

Slowly, Sam turned and made his way down the aisle of the bus.

At no time during this intervention did Mr. Cann begin asking Sam or the other boy what was going on (he dropped the content). By dropping the content, he directed the conversation to the need for the bus to keep moving. In this way, the three became allies in having to get off the bus together.

In close quarters, like a school bus, it is best to continue to use verbal intervention and to avoid physical contact. I have been in the "hot seat" like Mr. Cann. The only difference was that I was in a van full of eight adolescents, male and female, and the van was moving. My coworker was driving the fifteen-passenger van home from an off-grounds activity. A boy sitting in the back of the van started picking a fight with another boy. We were about fifteen minutes away from the secure facility, and it was up to me to go back and manage the scene.

I asked the other kids to move as far forward as possible, and they complied. Then I sat in the seat in front of the disruptive teen. I was well aware of the confined space and, thus, my potentially compromised safety. I engaged in a non-threatening conversation with the young man. Every time he made a derogatory remark about someone in the van, including me, I listened but didn't challenge him. Instead I would say, "You have been doing so well in the program."

I was able to keep the teen distracted, seated, and engaged until the vehicle stopped. I had to keep my cool and stay on my guard, since my charge was threatening to assault me, "I am going to go off on you and you can't stop me in this van," he said. I chose to take his words as indicative of his feelings of hopelessness, because his threats were random and apparently without any intent to affect change. I continued to implore him to hang in there. "You can keep it together. I know you can." I also knew that keeping the conversation steady was really the only choice. If the driver had to pull over and help me contain the teen, there would have been a risk of injury to all of us. My goal-oriented strategy worked and confirmed my opinion that hands-on may sometimes be a necessity, but more often than not, verbally engaging with an angry party is a viable option.

Hands-on Policies as Safeguards for the Innocent

A hands-on policy involves more than just the determination of when physical intervention is authorized. It addresses the need to protect workers and those they serve or care for from the abuse of physical force. People are vulnerable to abuse by workers who take revenge on them for acting out and resisting.

"Slapping Charges Lead to Probation" read the headline of the October 21, 1996 edition of the Greenfield, Massachusetts' newspaper, *The Recorder*. A nurses' aide had slapped a mildly retarded eighty-eight-year-old patient on the side of the head after the patient had punched the aide in the chest. This had occurred while the aide was moving the patient onto a geriatric chair.

Punishing a person is not a permissible use of hands-on. If you are feeling vengeful, it is best to leave the intervention and let someone else take over. An intervener who is unable to respond in a professional manner should step away from the conflict rather than victimize a person whose actions have spun out of control.

Modeling Alternatives to Violence

The intervener is the leader of the scene, setting the pace for the rest of the incident. When there has been an altercation, the leader must assess total scene safety. Immediately going in and breaking up a fight is not always the best choice for an intervener or the group at large. In a home, classroom setting, or any other site where hands-on may be used, interveners are role models. They should display what they deem to be good choices for managing a conflict.

When an intervener is talking softly to a student in crisis, giving specific instructions like "Come with me," and remaining calm, the message is clear to all onlookers: crisis intervention does not mean that the intervener has to accelerate to the same level of agitation as the person in crisis. The hands-on policy provides the guidelines for physical intervention, but the direction that the intervention takes is still up to the intervener(s).

Summary: Viability of a Universal Approach to Use of Force

Can there be a universal approach to the use of hands-on? It turns out that our society is already moving in that direction. Parents like Nick Carson, for example, who use excessive force on their children, are being called to task and charged with child abuse. Despite the parental right to govern one's children, there is still a need for accountability.

There is a view that guidelines are not necessary to govern private use of force—however, any one of the vignettes in this chapter could have been reworked as a parent-child scenario. While it is difficult enough for professional interveners to sustain a level of self-control when managing a conflict, emotions are particularly high when family members are involved. Irreconcilable emotional and physical damage can occur to another person when force is used arbitrarily or in the heat of the moment, especially by a family member.

Preventing unintentional injuries necessitates keeping a goal in mind when deciding to use hands-on. For instance, "To make the classroom scene safe, I will have to move Johnny out of the classroom or move his classmates away from Johnny." This goal defines the purpose behind using hands-on in order to establish scene safety. One undeniably bad option to achieve the goal of creating scene safety would be to swat Johnny on the side of the head or twist his arm until he cries out in pain to make him move. Only an unskilled intervener would rely on street fighting tactics and/or retaliatory acts to get Johnny's attention. Interveners trained on the limitations and risks of using hands-on understand the need to restrain their emotions and use only safe physical management techniques.

A parent or guardian can use the same model. For instance, Johnny's mother might say to herself, "To get Johnny to stop fighting with his brother, I will move him to his room or ask his brother to leave the living room." Leaving the emotional impact of Johnny's behavior temporarily out of the picture reduces the risk of his mother's wanting to lash out uncontrollably at him. She has only one goal in mind now: to make the scene safe. Discussing the conflict between Johnny and his brother can wait until both boys have settled down and his mother has been able to sort through her own emotions to make a decision that is based upon sound reasoning, not a knee-jerk reaction.

As useful as it is for managing conflict among non-family members, a Goal-Oriented Intervention also lessens the likelihood of hurting those we love and hold closest to our hearts.

The Model Relies on the Messenger

Tis the motive exalts the action.
Tis the doing, not the deed.

— Margaret Junkin Preston

Throughout history, messengers have crossed over battle lines at the request of one warring side to relay information to the other. They have had to face adversaries in wars that were likely not of their own making. The code of conduct for the commander was "not to shoot the messenger," so the saying goes, since he was just the courier, not the author of the message.

Unlike messengers, interveners act on their own accord. Though the two differ on many levels, there is common ground shared between the two roles. I would think, for instance, that a King's messenger put a very high value on being able to maintain neutrality and not get involved in an argument. Certainly messengers had everything to gain if they could step off the line of attack.

Interveners who follow the Goal-Oriented Intervention protocol as outlined in this book are, in my view, messengers of safety. They model self-control, drop the content, and step off the line. They are the standard bearers of what is deemed safe and convey clearly what is not safe. They hold a common goal for all when chaos is reigning—to be safe.

To be safe is an attainable goal. It is a universal truth—we all want to be safe. Safety is noted as the second baseline level in a hierarchy of needs in psychologist Abraham Maslow's often-cited 1943 paper entitled *A Theory of Human Development.* For even the most agitated person, safety isn't a hard sell. For an intervener, having her primary goal be safety takes the guesswork out of the eternal question "What should I do?"

The end goal of safety, though, isn't nearly enough for the intervention. Anyone can say "safety first". Actually attaining safety is another matter. A clear protocol is necessary to map out how the intervener garners safety. The crisis model sets the protocol. The attributes of a successful model are that it should be simply laid out—the steps easy to follow, attainable, and realistic for both interveners and those in crisis. The Response Crisis Intervention Model is all of the above, but it is worth noting that its simplicity is often met with disbelief.

"I look ridiculous when I exhale."

"I don't have time to pause."

"Ask, 'Am I safe?' That is too simplistic."

"Saying, 'thank you' is an intervention technique?"

"We don't resolve conflicts?"

"I shouldn't ask 'What's the problem?'"

These types of statements are quite common from participants of the Response Crisis Intervention Model seminars. There is often a sense of disbelief that telling an angry person to "Walk with me, please," or "Thank you for listening" —does actually work.

The funny thing is that looking back, I clearly recall thinking the same way. I used to believe that every crisis was unique and required a specific set of skills. I also thought being an intervener meant I had to make it all better, like I was vying for the "Do-Gooder Award" for crisis intervention. Make it all better meant resolve another person's crisis. I was twenty-one years old when I first started working in human services. By the time I was twenty-six, I was ready to hang it all up. You can only keep putting out other people's fires for so long, before that task becomes tiresome.

These days instead of feeling exhausted or fearful of conflict, I now embrace my role in conflict management. I still believe in having a tool bag of skills, but those skills are now tied into a very defined Goal-Oriented Intervention protocol.

I have never lost my faith in people and their desire to do the right thing for others who are in a state of distress and rage. Conflict may be a constant, but so is goodwill. Given the right tools and a clear goal, people will always be triumphant over chaos.

Conflict is scary. A reasonable amount of trepidation is not a bad thing to feel when deciding to intervene. However, keeping a level head and staying focused on the goal at hand—safety—will help thwart the fight or flight response.

In the end, order will always reign over chaos. The human race has been picking up the pieces after wars since the beginning of time. Families have the capacity to move on from violent tragedies. Chaos will have its moment and then order prevails—so goes the cycle.

It is not the actual chaos that I fear the most, but the loss of self-control that ignites the cycle of violence. We do, however, have the capacity to lead chaos towards order: it begins with a pause and exhale. Choose to bring order to conflict. Begin simply and stick to a set plan. It is our world, our choice, our task to lead chaos and not allow it to lead us. Be a messenger. Put safety first.

Acknowledgements

To all Response Instructors around the globe—Thank you.

You inspire me.

To the organizations and management teams who took the original chance on the Response Model and myself.

Your courage has effected change.

To Sensei Charles Gilliam much gratitude. Our twenty years and counting of teaching and practice at Wendell Aikido keeps me in "present time".

And as always, to family and friends who tolerated my absences and knew when to request my presence, during the revising of this book—lots of love.

About the Author

Alexandria A. Windcaller, M.H.S.A., is an internationally recognized consultant in the field of conflict management. She is the Founder and CEO of Response Training Programs, a staff development consulting firm specializing in crisis intervention trainings. She was a certified emergency medical technician for sixteen years. Her first edition of *Leading Chaos; An Essential Guide To Conflict Management* was published in 2002. She authored a column called "Off the Mat" for *Aikido Today Magazine* between 2000 and 2005. She is the Chief Instructor of Wendell Aikido, a martial arts dojo in western Massachusetts.

For more info on the author go to:
www.alexandriawindcaller.com